ASSEMBLIES
FOR SENSITIVE
ISSUES

Edited by
GERALD HAIGH

pfp

© 2002 pfp publishing limited

First published in Britain in 1997 by
pfp publishing limited
61 Gray's Inn Road
London WC1X 8TH

Written by Gerald Haigh.
Illustrations by Angela Lumley.
Cover and layout by Creative Media.
Cover photo by Getty Images/Photodisc.
Page design by Starfish.

Other assembly titles available from pfp include
• *Favourite Assemblies for Ages 4–7*
• *Favourite Assemblies for Ages 7–11*
• *The Primary Assembly Song Book*
• *All Year Round – Assemblies for Special Days and Celebrations*
• *Primary Assembly File*

pfp orders and customer service
Tel: 0870 241 0731
Web: www.pfp-publishing.com

Printed in the UK

ISBN 1 874050 57 0

A catalogue record for this book is available from the British Library.

CONTENTS

INTRODUCTION

Welcome to *Assemblies for Sensitive Issues*. For obvious reasons, we hope you will never have to use some parts of this publication. Other parts, however, may help you explore some of the most difficult and sensitive areas of primary school life.

Assemblies for Sensitive Issues deals with events that cause stress and unhappiness within the school community and materially affect the lives of pupils.

Using the file

All schools have experience of these events. The level of support, understanding and knowledge involved in dealing with such issues is extremely varied, but frequently headteachers use the framework of an assembly to help cope with the particular issue.

By nature, some tragedies are unpredictable and headteachers may be ill-prepared to hold

© pfp 2002 ISBN 1 874050 57 0 May be photocopied for use only within the purchasing institution **pfp**, 61 Gray's Inn Road, London WC1X 8TH

a well-thought out and effective assembly. For the more perennial sensitive issues, headteachers may lack knowledge or an ability to find the right words. *Assemblies for Sensitive Issues* is here to provide a fast, but considered, response. It is intended as part of a whole-school response to issues and not a complete answer – it is not a curriculum resource.

There are two basic reasons these assemblies might be used. One is when an immediate response to a particular event is needed. The other is when the assembly is part of a whole-school policy on, say, bullying. Obviously, these two overlap. An assembly on bullying, for example, can be used either as a fast response or as part of a whole-school approach.

Preparation

Assembly products from pfp have always needed as little as possible preparation. We've tried to stick to that principle in *Assemblies for Sensitive Issues* – we don't suggest resources that you'll have to search for. At the same time, it seems fair that for these topics, which by definition are challenging to handle, you should look at the assembly to see just how it might be tailored to fit your own needs.

After all, although every one of the topics we've covered may crop up in any school, its impact will be unique to you when it happens. Bullying is familiar and ubiquitous, but what you have to tackle is the sort of bullying that happens to your children in your school. And, if a child in your school dies, it will be a child personally known to you. All we can do, in all humility, is offer a set of frameworks that will help you at what will surely be a difficult time.

So, use our assemblies in whatever way seems appropriate to you. What we're aiming to do is give you a start when something's difficult to tackle.

How the file is structured

There are three sections and three appendices:
- Section 1 Responding to distressing incidents
- Section 2 Tackling school and community issues
- Section 3 Things that children worry about

The titles are self-explanatory. We need to stress, though, that the divisions can't be hard and fast and it would be a mistake to see them like that. It's not difficult to envisage a distressing incident becoming a whole-school issue that children worry about.

Appendix 1 contains information on children coping with divorce and separation. Appendix 2 provides information on bereaved children, and Appendix 3 contains a wealth of information, including support agencies, charities, publications and organisations, on a wide range of sensitive issues.

Appropriateness

Children's understandings and reactions to sensitive issues differ depending on their age and general experiences, so you will need to decide for yourself how appropriate an assembly is for your pupils.

Assembly format

All the assemblies follow the same format:
- a brief overview of the issue
- background information which identifies the key sensitivities and likely reactions of your pupils
- preparation needed before the assembly
- the assembly itself
- an option for either a prayer or thought.

The assembly itself sometimes has options and these, along with anything else that is not to be read out, are always shown in italics. The assembly can be read out as it is, or you can adapt some passages to fit your situation more closely.

Conclusion

Assemblies for Sensitive Issues sets out to:
- give reassurance and support in times of tragedy and stress
- offer comprehensive assembly coverage of sensitive issues
- help define a framework for considering how your school can cope with sensitive issues.

When you're at a loss for words, *Assemblies for Sensitive Issues* will give you support and help you say what needs said in times of tragedy and trauma.

The death of an adult

✦ Introduction

Sadly, adults do die during their working lives, sometimes suddenly and tragically. This assembly is to provide you with the information and support you would need should you be required to come to school one day ready to tell colleagues and pupils about the sudden loss of someone who works in the school. It is not only suitable for you to use following the death of a teacher, but following the death of any adult who is closely involved with the school, the staff and the pupils.

The assembly is the first of two that give you support in such an event. This first assembly helps cope with the immediate aftermath of such a tragedy. The second assembly (see page 9), is more reflective and offers a simple way of celebrating the deceased person's life.

It requires some brief preparation – see 'Before the assembly' below.

Aims:

The aims of this assembly are to

- dispel rumour and conjecture

- reassure children that there will be continuity in the school

- help those pupils who are seriously affected to take a more rational approach to the bereavement.

✦ Background

Many staff and pupils will be affected by the death. Where another staff member is very upset you may consider sending them home. Some pupils who did not know the member of staff well may be only slightly affected, whereas others who were closer will clearly be more so.

All those who are affected will be feeling a sense of bewilderment, shock and perhaps anger, especially if the death has been sudden. For the pupils most closely associated with the deceased person there could be a feeling of disbelief, and only later will they come to really understand that the person will not be coming back to school. This will be particularly true in the case of the class of a teacher who has died, and also of younger pupils. However, very young pupils (in general, those aged 5–7) tend to have little concept of death, and so it is less suitable to address such an event with them in this way. For this reason this assembly is recommended for use with 7–11 year olds.

This first assembly should not be long. It should be an initial step – just your first words, until you can decide with colleagues what is appropriate for the school to do in the medium and long term.

The tone of your approach is crucial. Deal with the tragedy openly – do not leave it to be something whispered about in the playground. (If assembly is usually late in the day, but children are already talking about the death, then bring it forward.) However, grief and nervousness – when it is difficult to find the

The death of an adult

right words and the right approach – can make a person say inappropriate things in an unexpected tone of voice. For this reason, the assembly that follows is intended to help you plan what to say and how to say it. You might not, of course, follow the text and actions exactly, but they show you a way forward, and are there if you find yourself at a loss for words.

(There are further notes on bereavement in Appendix 2, page 146, and organisations from which you can get further help and advice are listed under Appendix 3, Bereavement on pages 150–151.)

✦ Before the assembly

First, gather the following information and write it down. Do so, even if you think you know it, because you may be upset and forget things when you are speaking in assembly.

- The person's name.

- The names of his or her family – husband or wife, sons and daughters (use first names).

- Where he or she died (eg. in X hospital or at home).

- When he or she died (eg. this morning, yesterday afternoon, last night).

Make a photocopy of these details. Keep one copy with you and one on your desk. (Again, you may be upset and mislay your notes.)

Even though this is only your initial response to the event, and as such will be brief, if possible tell the person's family that you are going to mention him or her in assembly. You can also let them know that you would like to meet with them at a later date, to see if there is anything further that can be done in school.

Decide whether to include a colleague in the assembly and, if so, speak to him or her as soon as possible. If you are a relatively new headteacher, for example, and the colleague who has died was at your school for a long time, someone else may be able to say a few more personal words. A gesture like this will be much appreciated. Make sure that the person understands that you want something brief – a personal memory, a thought from a long-standing colleague. Do not hand over the whole assembly, however. You are the headteacher, and the staff look to you.

Even if you have already talked informally to most colleagues, gather them all together – perhaps delaying the morning bell for a few minutes. Include all the support staff you can, too. Ask the deputy or another colleague to perform playground duty.

Make a brief but dignified and quite formal announcement. In an informally organised school this may feel awkward at first, but after a word or two you will realise that it is appropriate and is appreciated as an important mark of respect. It will also signal to the staff what the tone of the school's immediate response will be, and serve as a preview for them of how you will handle the assembly. Staff look to the head in times of difficulty and you must appear steady, dignified and sure of what to do.

The following are points you might include.

- Factual information about the place and time of death.

- An expression of sadness and shock (if appropriate).

The death of an adult

- Sympathy for the family of the deceased – name the family (spouse, partner, children, etc.) and any close friends on the staff.

- Information on any actions you've taken so far, such as talking with the family or others close to the deceased person.

- The reason for holding a school assembly straightaway – because the children will be talking and whispering and you want the sad news out in the open.

- Information on what you are going to do immediately in terms of the assembly and its participants – this is particularly important if you're going to ask a colleague to speak in the assembly. Make it clear that the assembly will be brief, and that the tone will be quiet and thoughtful – much the same as the announcement you have made.

- Information on any changes to that day's arrangements as a result of the death.

- Any plans for a letter home (a copy of which should be sent separately to staff, so they know what is being said).

Thank staff in advance for their support.

📖 The assembly

Be gentle, but factual.

Sadly, I now have to tell you what some of you already know, that *(name of person)*, our **teacher/school helper** died *(say when and where as appropriate)*.

We all feel very sad at the thought that we will not see *(name)* again. All of us have many memories of **him/her**. Some of you knew **him/her** very well, and will be very upset

today. All of you will feel sad that a member of our school family has left us in this way. I have my own memories of **him/her**. *(Say a few very brief things about his or her character and personality.)*

What I want you to remember, though, is that however sad we are here in school, the people who will miss **him/her** most are the members of **his/her** own family *(name them, if appropriate)*. Let's think very specially of them.

Optional Now I am going to ask *(name of colleague)* to say a few words. Like *(name of deceased)*, **he/she** has been here for a long time – longer than I have – and **he/she** would like to add just a few thoughts.

After your colleague has spoken, continue as follows.

It's sometimes hard to understand why someone dies unexpectedly, but you should all know that *(name of deceased)* would have wanted us all to carry on in school and keep up with our work, have fun and enjoy our time here. That's what **he/she** did every day **he/she** was here. You might be feeling very sad or unhappy about what's happened – that's quite right and it's how most of us feel when someone we know dies. But you should also be pleased that you knew *(name)* and that **he/she** helped us so much in class and in school.

Some of you, and your parents, may want to know what we in school are going to do to remember *(name)*. It's very early days yet, and I will talk again to all of you about that later, when we have had time to think about it carefully. I will also be sending a letter home to tell your parents what has happened.

We'll finish for now with a **prayer/special thought** to help us in this sad time.

The death of an adult

☀ A prayer

Dear God, *(name)* worked in this school and was our friend whom we loved and now see no more. Help us at this sad time to remember all the good times and care **he/she** shared with us.

(If appropriate) We thank you for the hard work of the doctors and nurses who kept up **his/her** spirits and made **him/her** comfortable.

Please, God, help **his/her** family *(name them)*. Their loss is difficult for us to imagine, and things must look very dark for them. Please bring some light in their darkness. Amen.

☀ A thought

(Name of person) worked in this school and was our friend whom we loved and now see no more. Let's remember all the time **he/she** spent with us, and all the good times and care **he/she** shared with us.

(If appropriate) I'd like us to be thankful for the wonderful courage that **he/she** showed in **his/her** illness, and for the hard work of the doctors and nurses who kept up **his/her** spirits and made **him/her** comfortable.

Above all, let's remember **his/her** family *(name them)*. Their loss is difficult for us to imagine, and things must look very dark for them. In time, perhaps there will be some light in their darkness. Let's all try to help them and support them until then.

Memorial for an adult

✦ Introduction

This assembly deals further with the issues raised by the death of an adult connected with the school. It follows on from the assembly on page 5 and provides a framework for a more considered remembrance to be held some time after the death. It requires some preparation – see 'Before the assembly' below.

Aims:

The aims of this assembly are to

- offer a celebration and remembrance for the life of the person

- share some fond thoughts and memories of the person

- help children towards the acceptance of death, and to confirm its permanence

- show that memories can be supportive, and can be retained for as long as we wish

- remind the school of the contribution the person made to school life.

✦ Background

It is advisable for this assembly to take place at least two months after the death has occurred – perhaps the following term. This gives time for family and friends to begin to come to terms with the bereavement and for a considered remembrance assembly to be prepared.

If possible, make the assembly a special event, not combined with general announcements or other school matters.

Be aware that some children may become tearful during the assembly. Allow expressions of grief and decide what you will do should this happen (for example, whether to have a member of staff quietly take those pupils out of the assembly). This is less likely to happen in this assembly than in the address you gave immediately after the death, however, especially as the nature of this assembly is a positive and celebratory one. Using an appropriate tone and appropriate memories will help children realise and participate in this.

Also be aware that some members of staff may find the assembly moving.

✦ Before the assembly

Optional You will need a candle and something to light it with.

Invite close relatives to join you in the assembly, and ask them if they would like to make a contribution. (They may have a few words to say to the school or like to do a reading as suggested below.) If they do wish to be present, let them know in advance exactly what you are planning to say.

Find out whether the deceased had a favourite piece of music which you can play in the assembly. Or choose a calm, reflective piece of music you feel is appropriate to play in the background for a few moments' silent thought. (For example, Satie's *Gymnopodie II*.)

Memorial for an adult

Also find out if he or she had a favourite piece of writing. If so, decide who will read it out (it could be read out by a relative who would like to take part), and if appropriate, reproduce it on an OHT or in a service sheet.

Think about, and note down, any links you can mention between the music and the writing, and the person.

Ask others who knew the person for short tributes which you can note down and include in the assembly.

Ask children who knew the deceased to write some short pieces of their own about him or her. This may already have been done as part of the way either the whole school, or a class that was particularly close to the person, decided to deal with the death – if this is the case, choose the most appropriate pieces. Decide whether to read them yourself or whether to ask the children to do so. Make sure these children are well prepared and know that the assembly is a celebration and not a time for sadness or tears.

Find out as much as you can about the person's life. Note down a brief biography to tell to the assembly, including his or her contributions to school life.

Brief your staff before the assembly.

• Ask them to tell their classes the purpose of the assembly beforehand – that you are all going to take part in a positive celebration of the person's memory. Remind them to be careful with the tone in which they say this, in order to ensure that the children approach the assembly in a quiet and respectful mood.

• Let them know what you have decided to do, should any children become emotional. Mention that it's important to allow the children to express their grief, and ask them to cope quietly with such children, preferably by providing extra attention and physical contact such as putting hands on shoulders or a hug. Also let them know, although you're not expecting this to be necessary, in what case a child should be taken out of the assembly and, if appropriate, who by.

📖 The assembly

Optional *Light the candle and keep it burning at the front of the hall throughout the assembly.*

Our assembly today is a special one to remember *(name of deceased)*. It is not so long ago *(give the date)* that I called you together to tell you that *(name)* had died. You will remember how sad and shocked many of us were that day, especially those of you who knew *(name)* very well.

A little time has passed now. We are still sad. And those people who knew *(name)* best – **his/her** family and close friends – are just as sad as they were then, because the loss of someone you love is a big and difficult thing to bear.

But we've had some time to think about *(name)*, and I thought it would be a good idea for us to come into assembly again and share our different memories of *(name)* and talk about the different things that **he/she** meant to different people in our school community.

When a person dies, the feeling we have is one of loss. And the closer we were to the person, the worse the feeling is. We have to try to come to terms with the fact that the person

Memorial for an adult

we have lost is never coming back – that we are never going to see **him/her** again. That really is a very difficult thing to do. But we can always remember the person – we can look at pictures, and we can make pictures in our minds.

So, let's do some remembering. First, though, just to focus our minds, we'll sit quietly and play a piece of music that *(name)* liked very much. As you listen, make your own pictures of **him/her** in your mind. Try to remember actual events, not just vague things. Think of *(name)* doing something that you remember on a particular occasion.

Play the music as a background to the otherwise silent assembly. After a few minutes, continue. If possible, briefly mention any links between the deceased and the music that is playing, and then continue with the following.

Perhaps our memories are a bit clearer now. Let's make them clearer still with a few memories from some more people who knew *(name)*. Here are some from people I have spoken to.

Read out the memories.

And, of course, you have memories too. You've all just been thinking about them. Let's listen to the things that some of you wrote when you were asked to remember *(name)*.

Either read them yourself or ask the children to read them.

These are good memories, and although *(name)* is not coming back, the memories will stay for as long as you want them to. You can

bring them back into your mind whenever you want to think about **him/her**.

Let me just tell you some more about *(name)* – things that many of you may not know.

Give a brief biography. Make a special point of including his or her contributions to school life.

Optional *Include the following two paragraphs if relatives are present.*

The closer you were to *(name)*, of course, the greater the loss. And as I said earlier, for some people, like **his/her** family, the loss is so great that it seems unbearable. None of us can really make that easier.

We haven't shared our memories just because we want to make you feel better. We just want you to know that we remember **him/her**, and that we are here thinking of you as well as thinking of **him/her**.

Optional. *If a relative has chosen to take part in the assembly, invite them to make their contribution at this point.*

Optional. Now, before we finish, here is one of *(name)*'s favourite pieces of writing.

Optional. *Show the OHT or refer to the service sheet if you have decided to produce the piece in one of these ways.*

Before I *(or whoever has been decided upon)* read it, let me tell you why we have chosen it *(as with the music, briefly talk about the link between the writing and the deceased person)*.

Memorial for an adult

Let's end our assembly now with all of our good memories and a **prayer/thought**.

✲ A prayer

Dear God, we remember *(name)* today. We want to keep good memories of **him/her**, and to be thankful for the good things that **he/she** did for us here. We are grateful, and we want to give thanks, and we also want to celebrate **his/her** life.

We know that death comes to everyone, but we also know that every time somebody dies, there are people for whom the loss is difficult to bear. We ask you to comfort those who are specially upset, and we ask you to keep their feelings in our minds and help us understand just a little of what it means to lose a loved one. Amen.

✲ A thought

Death is loss, and loss is painful to those who are left behind. Good memories cannot make up for losing someone you care a great deal about, but they do provide something you can keep hold of, and think about, when you feel particularly sad. We can always remember *(name)*, we can be grateful for all the things **he/she** did for us, and we can celebrate the life that **he/she** shared with us and many other people.

The death of a child after a long illness

✦ Introduction

This assembly deals with the death of a child who has been ill for some time. It is the first of two that give you support in such an event. This first assembly helps you cope with the immediate aftermath of such a tragedy. The second assembly (see page 21), designed to take place at a later date – is more reflective and offers a simple way of celebrating the child's life.

It requires some brief preparation – see 'Before the assembly' below. It's possible that such a tragedy is expected, in which case you could carry out the preparation some time ahead of the assembly if you wished.

Aims:

The aims of this assembly are to

- give brief factual information about what has happened

- dispel some of the children's worst fears and sadness

- offer the school's sympathy and support to the bereaved parents.

✦ Background

Even though it might have been expected, the death of a child after a long illness is always a tragedy for a school community. Often the child's family will have been struggling on their own with the tragedy of the illness, but many in the school community will also be aware of what has been happening.

Close friends of the child may have been giving him or her support and will be quite badly affected when the death occurs. If there are such children in your school you might need to offer them specific help in coming to terms with the bereavement.

All those who are affected will be feeling a sense of bewilderment, shock and perhaps anger. For the pupils most closely associated with the deceased child there could be a feeling of disbelief and only later will they come to really understand that the child will not be coming back to school. It's not uncommon for some children to react in seemingly inappropriate ways, such as laughing or giggling. Be prepared for this and deal with the children sympathetically.

This will be particularly true in the case of younger pupils, the very youngest of whom (in general those aged 5–7) tend to have little concept of death. It may not always be suitable to address such an event with them in this way, but in the case of it being one of their friends or a member of their class, you may feel that it is appropriate to do so.

In certain circumstances – for example if your school is a large one – you may feel that it is not appropriate to hold this assembly with everyone present. If so, it is also suitable to be used with a particular year group or class.

The death of a child after a long illness • page 1 of 4

The death of a child after a long illness

This first assembly should not be long. It should be a first step until you can decide with colleagues what other things you and the school can, or should, do in the medium or long term.

The tone of your approach is crucial. Deal with the tragedy openly – do not leave it to be something whispered about in the playground. (If assembly is usually late in the day, but children are already talking about the death, then bring it forward.) However, grief and nervousness – when it is difficult to find the right words and the right approach – can make a person say inappropriate things in an unexpected tone of voice. For this reason, the assembly that follows is intended to help you with what to say and how to say it. You might not, of course, follow the text and actions exactly, but they show you a way forward, and are there if you find yourself at a loss for words.

During the assembly, be aware that a close friend or group of friends of the child may be tearful. Allow expressions of grief and decide whether or not it is appropriate to have a member of staff quietly take those pupils out of the assembly in case the whole event becomes too emotional.

(There are further notes on bereavement in Appendix 2, page 146, and organisations from which you can get further help and advice are listed under Appendix 3, Bereavement on pages 150–151.)

✦ Before the assembly

First, gather the following information and write it down. Do so, even if you think you know it, because you may be upset and forget things when you are speaking in assembly.

- The child's name.

- The names of his or her family – parents and brothers and sisters (use the parents' first names, which will be familiar to some of the children).

- A reminder of the nature of the illness – though you might decide not to go into this in the first assembly.

- Where he or she died (eg. in X hospital or at home).

- When he or she died (eg. this morning, yesterday afternoon, last night).

Also note down a few personal thoughts about the child's personality and character that you can mention.

Make a photocopy of these details. Keep one copy with you and one on your desk. (Again, you may be upset and mislay your paper.)

Even though this is only your initial response to the event, and as such will be brief, if possible tell the child's parents that you are going to mention their child in assembly. You can also let them know that you would like to meet with them at a later date to see if there is anything further that can be done in school to remember their child.

The death of a child after a long illness

Even if you have already talked informally to most colleagues, gather them all together – perhaps delaying the morning bell slightly. Include support staff and kitchen staff, too. Ask the deputy or another colleague to perform playground duty.

Make a brief, but dignified, and quite formal announcement. In an informally organised school, this may feel awkward at first, but after a word or two you will realise that it is appropriate, and is appreciated as an important mark of respect. It will also be a signal to the staff as to what the tone of the school's immediate response will be. It will also be a preview for them of how you will handle the forthcoming assembly. Staff look to the headteacher in times of difficulty and you must appear steady, dignified and sure of what to say and do.

The following are points you might include.

- Factual information about the place and time of death.

- Brief details of the child's illness, the medical staff, and hospital who tried to alleviate the suffering.

- Sympathy with the child's family in their time of grief (use their names if appropriate).

- Information about any contact you may have had with the family.

- The reason for holding a school assembly straightaway – because the children will be talking and whispering and you want the sad news out in the open.

- Information about the assembly – that it will be brief, and that the tone will be quiet and thoughtful. Tell them what you have decided to do should any child or group of children become tearful, for example in what event

they should quietly be taken out of the assembly by a particular member of staff. Also mention that it is important to allow the children to express their grief.

- Any information you know already about what is being planned in school. Reinforce the fact that the approach will be a collective and sensitive one and will take into account the feelings of the family. Staff may have ideas about what could be done – let them know that you will arrange a meeting to discuss these at a later date.

- Any plans for a letter home (a copy of which should be sent separately to staff so they know what is being said).

📖 The assembly

Be gentle, but factual.

You all know that *(name of child)* has been very ill. Sadly, I now have to tell you what some of you already know, that *(name)* died peacefully in **hospital/at home** yesterday with **his/her** family around **him/her**.

We all feel very sad at the thought that we will not see *(name)* again. Some of you knew **him/her** very well, and will be very upset today. All of you will feel sad that a member of our school family has left us in this way. All of us have many memories of **him/her**. *(Say a few very brief things about the child's character and personality.)*

What I want you to remember is that however sad we are here in school, the people who will miss *(name)* most are the members of **his/her** family – **his/her** mum and dad and brothers and sisters *(name them)*. Let's think very specially of them.

The death of a child after a long illness

Some of you, and your parents, may want to know whether we are going to do something special to remember *(name)* by. We will think about that in the near future and we will let you all know what we plan to do. You will understand that we will want to talk to *(name)*'s family first and this will take some time. Meanwhile, keep them in your thoughts.

Let's help ourselves to do that with a **prayer/special thought**.

☀ A prayer

Dear God, we bring before you *(name)*, a pupil of this school, our friend whom we loved and now see no more. We thank you for the time **he/she** spent with us, and we ask you to help us to think of the cheerful times before **he/she** fell ill. We also thank you for the wonderful courage that **he/she** showed in **his/her** long illness, and for the hard work of doctors and nurses who kept up **his/her** spirits and made **him/her** comfortable.

Above all, we remember *(name)*'s family – *(name them again)*. Their loss is difficult for us to imagine, and things must look very dark for them. In time, perhaps there will be some light in their darkness. Help them and support them until then. Amen.

☀ A thought

(Name) was our friend who we loved but who we now see no more. *(Name)* was very brave, and while **he/she** lived was a great example to us all. *(If appropriate)* I'd like us to be thankful for the wonderful courage that **he/she** showed in **his/her** illness, and for the hard work of the doctors and nurses who made **him/her** comfortable.

Although we are sad and miss **him/her**, let's remember the cheerful and good times **he/she** had and that we spent together. Let's also remember **his/her** family *(name them)*. Their loss is difficult for us to imagine, and things must look very dark for them. In time, perhaps, there will be some light in their darkness. Let's all try to help them and support them until then.

© **pfp** 2002 ISBN 1 874050 57 0 May be photocopied for use only within the purchasing institution **pfp**, 61 Gray's Inn Road, London WC1X 8TH

The sudden death of a child

· · · · · © pfp 2002 ISBN 1 874050 57 0 ·

✦ Introduction

A primary school in the Midlands has, within the last ten years, suffered the sudden death of three pupils – two from road accidents on a nearby dual carriageway which children often cross as a shortcut, and one from a tragic shooting accident involving another child. This is exceptional, but it underlines the fact that on virtually any morning one or more schools in the country could be gathering for assembly in the knowledge that a pupil has died suddenly during the previous twelve hours or so. This assembly helps you cope with such a situation and requires some short preparation.

(There is also a second, more reflective, assembly on page 21, designed to take place at a later date and to offer a simple way of celebrating the child's life. This may or may not not be appropriate, depending on the nature of the death, so please approach it with careful thought. If you are not sure whether it would be appropriate, the notes on page 21 may help you decide.)

Aims:

The aims of this assembly are to

- give expression and words to otherwise unfocused and inarticulate distress

- provide information within acceptable limits

- reassure the children that life within school will go on

- give notice of further acts of remembrance when a little time has gone by.

✦ Background

In some cases the death may have come through violent means. Be aware that this will make it especially hard for children to accept.

Whatever the cause, many children will be feeling very upset and bewildered by the tragedy, while others – who may not have known the child concerned – will be little affected or simply curious. Frequently, rumours about the tragedy will be discussed in class and in the playground, and some children can become frightened and confused if these are not dealt with quickly.

Depending on the mood and size of your school, you may wish to make this an assembly for an appropriate class or classes only, the child's year group or the whole school. Those children who knew the child well will need to be given an opportunity to express their feelings within a class or a smaller group. Many children will want to talk about their friend. Others may need to express their feelings through non-verbal mediums, such as drawings or with clay. Discussions with staff will help you decide what is most appropriate.

A special friend may need to have extra care taken of him or her and, perhaps, to be looked after out of the assembly if emotions are running very high. You may also need to offer him or her specific help in coming to terms with the bereavement in the following period of time.

This assembly should not be long. It should be a first step, until you can decide with colleagues what other things you and the school can, or should, do in the medium or long term.

The sudden death of a child

The tone of your approach is crucial. Deal with the tragedy openly – do not leave it to be something whispered about in the playground. (If assembly is usually late in the day but children are already talking about the death, then bring it forward.) However, grief and nervousness – when it is difficult to find the right words and the right approach – can make a person say inappropriate things in an unexpected tone of voice. For this reason, the assembly that follows is intended to help you with what to say and how to say it. You might not, of course, follow the text and actions exactly, but they show you a way forward, and are there if you find yourself at a loss for words.

During the assembly, be aware that a close friend or group of friends of the child may be tearful. Allow expressions of grief, and decide whether or not it is appropriate to have a member of staff quietly take those pupils out of the assembly, in case the whole event becomes too emotional.

(There are further notes on bereavement in Appendix 2, page 146, and organisations from which you can get further help and advice are listed under Appendix 3, Bereavement on pages 150–151.)

✦ Before the assembly

First, gather the following information and write it down. Do so, even if you think you know it, because you may be upset and forget things when you are speaking to assembly.

- The child's name.

- The names of his or her family – parents and brothers and sisters (use the parents' first names, which will be familiar to some of the children).

- Where he or she died (eg. in hospital or at home).

- When he or she died (eg. this morning, yesterday afternoon, last night).

You may find that it's appropriate to discuss why the child died (for example, because of the kind of injuries that he or she sustained in an accident), and you will need to be prepared to do this. Children need to know how death occurs, and that it is because of real, physical causes. Make notes that will help you with this.

Make a photocopy of these details. Keep one copy with you and one on your desk. (Again, you may be upset and mislay your notes.)

Even though this is only your initial response to the event and as such will be brief, if possible tell the child's parents that you are going to mention their child in assembly. You can also let them know that you would like to meet with them at a later date, to see if there is anything further that can be done in school to remember their child.

⬤ ⬤ ⬤ ⬤ ⬤ ⬤ ⬤ ⬤ ⬤ ⬤ ⬤ ⬤

Even if you have already talked informally to most colleagues, gather them all together – perhaps delaying the morning bell for a few minutes. Include support staff and kitchen staff, too. Ask the deputy or another colleague to perform playground duty.

Make a brief but dignified, and quite formal announcement. In an informally organised school, this may feel awkward at first, but after a word or two you will realise that it is appropriate and is appreciated as an important mark of respect. It will also be a signal to the staff what the tone of the school's immediate response will be. It will also be a preview for them of how you will handle the forthcoming assembly. Staff look

The sudden death of a child

to the headteacher in times of difficulty and you must appear steady, dignified and sure of what to say and do.

The following are points you might include.

- Factual information about the place and time of death.

- Brief details of the event that caused the child's death.

- Sympathy with the child's family in their time of grief (use their names if appropriate).

- Information about any contact you may have had with the family.

- The reason for holding a school assembly straightaway – because the children will be talking and whispering and you want the sad news out in the open.

- Information about the assembly – that it will be brief, and that the tone will be quiet and thoughtful. Tell them what you have decided to do should any child or group of children become tearful, for example in what event they should quietly be taken out of the assembly by a particular member of staff. Also mention that it is important to allow the children to express their grief.

- Information – if any – that you already know about what is being planned in school. Reinforce the fact that the approach will be a collective and sensitive one and will take into account the feelings of the family. Staff may have ideas about what could be done – let them know that you will arrange a meeting to discuss these at a later date.

- Any plans for a letter home (a copy of which should be sent separately to staff, so they know what is being said).

Choose a calm, reflective piece of music that you can play to begin the assembly, for example, Satie's *Gymnopodie II.*

📖 The assembly

Adopt a reassuring attitude (smile at the children as they come in). Play your chosen piece of music.

As many of you know by now, we have some dreadful news this morning. We have learned that our pupil and friend *(name of child)* has died. *(Give details of when, where and how – use your prompt sheet if necessary.)*

At the moment there is very little that any of us can say. We are filled with a whole mixture of feelings – we think of **him/her**, and that brings us a constant reminder that we are not going to see **him/her** again. For many of us this will seem almost too much to bear. Do not be ashamed of any of your thoughts – if you cry, that's perfectly alright. If you laugh when you think of some of the things **he/she** said and did, then that's alright too. If you want to laugh and cry at the same time, then we all understand that, too. And if you just want to remember **him/her** quietly, without speaking to others about **him/her**, then you can do that.

Events like this are always difficult to understand, and difficult to deal with, for us as adults as well as for you. So we all need each other. We need to help each other and support each other. We need to forget our own problems and quarrels and differences for a while, because what has happened to *(name)* and **his/her** family is so much greater than any difficulties that we might have.

Our feelings will be strong and difficult to bear, but we must try to think how much

The sudden death of a child

stronger these feelings are for **his/her** family *(say their names)*. We must think of them and keep them in our hearts.

Optional *(if you already know that this will happen)* I'll be writing to them on your behalf.

Again, optional *(if you already know that this will happen)* Later on, we will have another assembly at which we will try to remember *(name)* more fully, and think again of **his/her** family.

I won't say much more now, but let's do two things together. First, let's have a few moments of silence in which we can think of our own memories of *(name)* and our own thoughts about **his/her** family.

Leave the assembly in silence for a minute or so.

Now let's join together in a **prayer/thought**.

☀ A prayer

Dear God, help us to think for a while about *(name)*. Help, in particular, those of us who were **his/her** friends and who need to know your love is still with *(name)* and with us.

As the day goes on, we will come to realise that this really has happened, and that we will not be seeing **him/her** again. But we are left with memories of **him/her**, and they are good memories that in time we will come to treasure and be thankful for.

Most importantly, God, we pray for *(name)*'s family *(name them)*. We really cannot imagine what their feelings are today. All we can do is keep them in our hearts and minds, and trust that you will give them the strength to bear what seems to be almost unbearable. Amen.

☀ A thought

Let's think for a while about *(name)*.

When we think of **him/her** today we feel nothing but distress and disbelief that such a thing can have happened. As the day goes on, we will realise that it really has happened, and that we will not be seeing **him/her** again. But we are left with memories of **him/her**, and they are good memories that in time we will come to treasure and be thankful for.

Most importantly, let's think of *(name)*'s family *(name them)*. We really cannot imagine what their feelings are today. All we can do is keep them in our hearts and minds and trust that they will have the strength to bear what seems to be almost unbearable.

Memorial for a child

✦ Introduction

This assembly takes the form of a meditation for a pupil who has died. It is not to be held immediately (see pages 14 and 17 for assemblies to help you provide an immediate response), but is designed to be a more considered event to be held at a later date. Whether or not such an assembly is appropriate does depend to a large extent on the way in which a child has died – do think about this carefully. The notes at the start of the 'Background' section below may help you decide. It requires some preparation – see 'Before the assembly' below.

Aims:

The aims of this assembly are to

- offer a celebration and remembrance for the life of the child

- share some fond thoughts and memories of the child

- help children towards the acceptance of death, and to confirm (especially for younger children) its permanence

- show that memories can be supportive, and can be retained for as long as we wish

- remind the school of the contribution the child made to school life.

✦ Background

Think carefully about the nature of the child's death before deciding to go ahead with such an assembly as this one. In almost all cases in which a child has died after a prolonged illness, such an assembly probably is appropriate. It will be an event which in some ways everyone has been prepared for, and which many people in the school community have in some way participated in even before the death actually happened. The bravery of the child alone will make a celebration of him or her a special thing.

However, there are also circumstances in which such an assembly would not be recommended. Many of the ways in which a child may have died suddenly, for example, may bring back memories that it would be wiser to leave to fade.

It is advisable for this assembly to take place some time after the death has occurred – perhaps the following term, or even around six months later. This gives time for family and friends to begin to come to terms with the bereavement and for a considered remembrance assembly to be prepared.

If possible, make the assembly a special event, not combined with general announcements or other school matters. Keep it relatively brief – such an event ought not to be too drawn out and emotionally demanding.

Memorial for a child

Be aware that some children may become tearful during the assembly. Allow expressions of grief and decide what you will do should this happen (for example, whether to have a member of staff quietly take those pupils out of the assembly). This is less likely to happen in this assembly than in the address you gave immediately after the death, however, especially as the nature of this assembly is a positive and celebratory one. Using an appropriate tone and appropriate memories, will help children realise and participate in this.

✦ Before the assembly

You will need a candle and something to light it with.

Choose a calm and reflective – but not too solemn – piece of music that you can play to end the assembly. For example, Parry's *An English Suite – Air*.

Check whether any relatives want to be present or to take part and, if so, how. They may want to say a few words of their own, do a reading or would perhaps like a particular piece of music played. If this is the case, discuss the celebratory nature of the assembly with the person to make sure that the tone is appropriate. You may like to note down some thoughts about the link between the child and the piece of music or reading to help you introduce it, or to follow on from it.

Ask some children either from the child's class, or some who were his or her special friends, to write down some of the good memories they have about their friend which they will read out in assembly. These children should be well prepared and clearly told that this is a celebration of their friend and not a time for sadness or tears.

Brief your staff before the assembly.

- Ask them to tell their classes the purpose of the assembly beforehand – that you are all going to take part in a positive celebration of the child's memory. Remind them to be careful with the tone in which they say this, in order to ensure that the children approach the assembly in a quiet and respectful mood.

- Let them know what you have decided to do should any children become emotional. Mention that it's important to allow the children to express their grief, and ask them to cope quietly with such children, preferably by providing extra attention and physical contact, such as putting hands on shoulders or giving a hug. Also let them know that although you're not expecting this to be necessary, in what case a child should be taken out of the assembly and, if appropriate, who by.

📖 The assembly

Assemble in silence. Light the candle and keep it burning at the front of the hall throughout the assembly.

Let's sit in silence for a moment and remember why we are here today. We are here to fondly remember *(name of child)*, and to celebrate the life we were lucky enough to share with **him/her**.

Now let's give more shape to our thoughts. Let's each of us call to mind a memory of *(name of child)*. Let it be a good memory. *(Allow just a beat of silence between each of these thoughts.)*

A moment of laughter that you shared with **him/her**, perhaps.

A kind and thoughtful action that **he/she** did.

A time when **he/she** was feeling sad and a bit down and something happened to cheer **him/her** up.

A time when **he/she** was in class, with a frown on **his/her** face, working hard to solve a problem.

Memories like these are very clear for so many of us, and they bring on a mixture of feelings. Obviously there is sadness. There is great sadness for *(name)*'s family, but there is also sadness for us here who loved and respected **him/her**.

But there is not just reason for us to be sad. There is reason for us to be thankful too. We can be thankful that we knew *(name)* so well. We can be thankful for the time that we spent together, and all the good memories we have. And when we call up memories of **him/her** it reminds us that friendship stays with us even when our friend is not with us any more.

Now, some friends who knew *(name)* very well are going to tell us some of their special memories. *Invite the chosen children to read their prepared pieces.*

Optional *Say at the end of each reading* God, we thank you for this memory. May it stay in our hearts as a reminder of your love.

Optional *If a relative of the child has chosen to take part in the assembly, invite him or her to make his or her contribution at this point.*

I'd like to thank everyone who has shared their memories today – it's certainly helped me remember what a special child *(name)* was. Now let's close our eyes a moment for a **prayer/special thought**.

☀ A prayer

Dear God, you know that there is much sadness in our hearts today, and that some people are carrying more grief than they feel able to bear. Please give them the strength to meet each day as it comes. Please especially help *(name)*'s family come to terms with their loss, and let them know that we here in school are thinking about them.

But also, dear God, we are thankful that we knew *(name)*. We thank you for **his/her** presence among us, for **his/her** courage and cheerfulness and good example. Thank you for all the good things **he/she** achieved in **his/her** life, and for giving us all the good memories, which will stay with us, and which we can celebrate. Amen.

☀ A thought

We know that there is much sadness in our hearts today, and that some people are carrying more grief than they feel able to bear. We know that there is no easy way to stop this. Let us hope we can all find the strength to meet each day as it comes. Let's especially wish for that strength for *(name)*'s family, who are always in our thoughts.

Memorial for a child

But at the same time as the sadness, let's be grateful that we all knew *(name)*. Let's be thankful for **his/her** presence among us, for **his/her** courage and cheerfulness and good example. And let's be thankful for all the good things **he/she** achieved in **his/her** life, and for all the good memories we have, which will stay with us and which we can always celebrate.

 ## To end the assembly

There's just one final thing we can be thankful for. I want us to be thankful for this time we have had together, today, in memory of our friend *(name)*. **His/her** life may have been short, but it was packed with good things which **his/her** family, friends and all of us in school were able to share. Let's leave this assembly with happy thoughts and feelings about *(name)*.

Play your chosen piece of music as the children leave the assembly.

The serious injury of a child in a road accident

✦ Introduction

On rare occasions children are injured on the way to or from school. This assembly gives you an immediate response to such a situation. It requires some brief preparation – see 'Before the assembly' below.

Aims:

The aims of this assembly are to

- give facts and allay rumours

- provide (if possible) a hopeful message about the injured child's progress

- talk about the care and support needed for his or her parents and family

- reinforce a safety message.

✦ Background

When a relatively serious accident happens to a child in your school, emotions are likely to run high among pupils in the same class or year group as the accident victim. Depending on the size of the school there may also be a strong reaction in other classes and year groups. Certainly the word will go around about what has happened and children may be frightened – some may even have witnessed the accident.

Use the assembly as a way of reinforcing the safety message, but take care. The danger is that you will give the impression that it was in some way the child's fault. For example, even though you don't directly say, 'If only he or she had waited for the lollipop lady', your message may be received in that way.

Make this part – or all – of your usual assembly. Try not to create a special atmosphere of drama or concern.

✦ Before the assembly

Make sure you have as many of the facts as you can. These should include

- the names of the child's immediate family

- the hospital where he or she has been taken

- the place where the accident happened.

📖 The assembly

Most of you will know by now that *(name of child)* had an accident *(on the way to or from school)* **yesterday/today**. As yet, it is not absolutely clear what happened, but it seems that **he/she** was knocked down on *(name the road or location)*.

Adapt the following paragraph as appropriate to your situation.

Some of **his/her** bones were broken, and **he/she** is at present in *(name the ward and the hospital)*.

The serious injury of a child in a road accident

His/her injuries are quite serious, and I expect **he/she** is feeling pretty miserable and probably hurts a lot. It's a terrible shock to be hit by a vehicle, and it will take **him/her** some time to get over it.

The good news is that **he/she** is going to get better, and will be back among us when everything is healed up enough for **him/her** to get around. Until then we'll think about *(name)* a lot, and be grateful for the fact that **he/she** has come through this accident in such a way that **he/she** will be able to get better.

Pause.

● ● ● ● ● ● ● ● ● ● ●

Just for a quiet moment let's think now about our friend *(name)*, lying injured in hospital this morning. It's at times like this that we realise how important doctors and nurses are and how it's their skill and commitment that will help bring *(name)* back to us here in school.

We know that **he/she** has plenty of courage and cheerfulness, and with all our thoughts being with **him/her** let's hope that **he/she** can be strong enough to bear the discomfort of being in hospital. Let's remember **his/her** family too *(name them, if appropriate)*. It's a very anxious time for them – they must be upset and worried. Let's hope they have strength and courage too. May each day bring more strength and healing.

Pause.

● ● ● ● ● ● ● ● ● ● ●

We don't know exactly how *(name)*'s accident happened, or whether anybody was at fault. But **his/her** injury reminds us of what we already know – that the roads around our school are dangerous. A small human body is no match for a big metal car weighing more than a tonne. Please remember that. Also remember that car drivers can be careless, or distracted, or full of their own thoughts, and they may not be ready for you if you do something they are not expecting.

Let's run through, again, some of the ways you can keep yourself safe.

Run through the rules about crossing roads, using the pelican, using the lollipop person and so on, as appropriate to your situation.

● ● ● ● ● ● ● ● ● ● ●

Each day many people are injured on our roads. A few, very sadly, are even killed. Each day there are people who set off happily to work and school and end up in accidents. Let's **pray for/think of** all the people who are out using the roads today – that they will all return home safely.

And especially today, let's also **pray for/think of** *(name)*, and hope that **he/she** recovers and is back with us soon.

© **pfp** 2002 ISBN 1 874050 57 0 May be photocopied for use only within the purchasing institution **pfp**, 61 Gray's Inn Road, London WC1X 8TH

The serious injury of a child in a road accident

☀ A prayer

Dear God, we remember all the people out and about on the roads today. Children going to and from school, men and women driving to and from work, men and women driving lorries and vans to deliver the things we need, bus and taxi drivers, motor cycle messengers, cyclists, walkers, shoppers with baby buggies – all who have to share our busy roads. Keep all of them safe, so that they can return to their families. Help them to keep thinking ahead about what might happen. Help them just to stop before taking a careless action.

And especially, please look after *(name)* too. Help **him/her** to get better and be back with us as soon as possible. Amen.

☀ A thought

Let's remember all the people out and about on the roads today – children going to and from school, men and women driving to and from work, men and women driving lorries and vans to deliver the things we need, bus and taxi drivers, motor cycle messengers, cyclists, walkers, shoppers with baby buggies – all who have to share our busy roads. We hope that all of them are safe, so that they can return to their families. Help them to keep thinking ahead about what might happen. Help them just to stop before taking a careless action.

But let's think specially of *(name)* too, and hope that our thoughts help **him/her** get better and come back to us as soon as possible.

☀ To end the assembly

Now let's get about our own business in school. We will all, of course, keep thinking about *(name)* and hoping that **he/she** gets better really soon. When I have more news I promise I will come round and let you know.

Serious damage to the school by fire, flood or vandalism

✦ Introduction

This assembly provides a focused response to cope with the destruction of the whole school or part of the school by fire, or its severe damage by flood. It is also written to deal with the situation where extensive damage has been caused by intruders. It requires some preparation – see 'Before the assembly' below.

Aims:

The aims of this assembly are to

- give facts

- give reassurance

- allay immediate fears

- explain future communication

- explain that cleaning up will be done by professionals.

✦ Background

As headteacher, your first concern in such a situation is to establish that the school is safe. However, the next priority must be the children and their parents.

When pupils and parents arrive at school to find that damage has been done, it is easy for you to be so bogged down with your own concerns and problems that you simply send somebody to the gate to send them away until further notice. However, it is important that you do give them an immediate and personal response, as they will have considerable worries, questions and concerns and may even be quite emotional.

So, hold an assembly as soon as is practical. Even if the school is too badly damaged to be used and is to be temporarily closed, or if some pupils are to be sent home, hold a short meeting with as many pupils and parents as you can gather together.

If at all possible, assemble in the school hall if it remains usable, as a familiar setting is preferable. If this is not possible, if there is a neighbouring school on the same site they will invariably help, or there may be a church or a civic hall nearby.

All the children, but the youngest ones in particular, need to be assured that they and all their friends at school are safe. They need to see their teachers and to be told that eventually they will all come together again. Give this priority in the assembly.

Children will also be concerned about their work and the fruits of all their efforts. They need to be reassured, and told that if things have been destroyed, they can make and create new examples of what has been damaged or lost.

Don't underestimate the feelings of parents and children. They will be anxious for facts, and also, probably, anxious to do something to help – if they don't ask you immediately what they can do, they soon will! They need to know what has happened and what is going to happen – in the absence of facts they will substitute rumour and gossip.

© **pfp** 2002 ISBN 1 874050 57 0 May be photocopied for use only within the purchasing institution **pfp**, 61 Gray's Inn Road, London WC1X 8TH

Serious damage to the school by fire, flood or vandalism • page 1 of 4

Serious damage to the school by fire, flood or vandalism

✦ Before the assembly

Make a note of all the facts that you already know

- the cause of the damage

- the extent of it

- alternative arrangements made for the day

- anything else that has to be done immediately.

Keep this note with you as a reminder – you will have a lot to think about and may forget some important points if they are not written down.

If at all possible, make it a priority to hold a staff meeting before the assembly. Cover these points with your staff.

- The facts – what has happened and what the arrangements for the immediate future are.

- Allocation of responsibilities. Staff need to feel they are helping. If the extent of the damage is not yet clear, set a time for a further meeting when it will be clear what needs to be done. Say that everyone will have something to do, and then keep that promise. Don't let information and participation gaps arise between senior staff and others.

- How you will keep in touch with children, parents and staff if anyone has to be dispersed.

In some ways, the message that you need to give to the staff is the same as the one you are giving the children. Reinforce the message that school is the people, not the building, and that it will continue in some form and will eventually resume, strengthened by the experience.

📖 The assembly

The atmosphere, with parents and children present, may be quite charged. Wait for, and encourage, quietness.

Let the quiet continue for a few moments. Then speak quietly and in a very steady voice – remember everyone is looking to you to set the tone.

Today is a very different sort of day – a sad and difficult day for all of us. We have had many assemblies in our school and most of them have been happy, but today we have a sad one. Why is that?

The answer is, of course, that our school has been badly damaged by *(explain the facts of the cause of the damage)*.

This is the damage that has been done. *(List it carefully as far as you know.)*

Optional *If there is doubt about the cause of the damage use the following paragraph – if the cause is clear then go to the next paragraph.*

Nobody knows whether it was done deliberately, or how it happened. All kinds of stories and rumours will go around, but we should not worry ourselves with finding out. If there is someone to blame, then the right people – the police – will find them. We have other things to do.

First, let me tell you that when I said that our school had been damaged, what I meant was that the building has been damaged. Because the school is really all of us – children, parents, staff and myself, of course. And we have not been damaged. Look at me! I am still just the same as I was yesterday. Look round at your teachers, and your friends. They are still the same, too.

Serious damage to the school by fire, flood or vandalism

If we lived in a hot country, we could all go out and find a shady tree and have our lessons together, and we would still be *(name of school)*. We could put our name board up there, and our school would go on in just the same way as usual, only outside instead of inside.

But sadly, we can't do that here. The sun doesn't shine every day in this country, and we have rain and too many other difficulties for us to work outside. So I have to tell you that *(part of)* our school will have to close for a while. *(Some of)* you will be asked to go home with your parents until we work out how we can carry on.

I will keep the time we are away from each other as short as I possibly can. I have all your names and addresses, and many of your brothers and sisters are in other classes here, or go to schools nearby *(adapt as appropriate)*, so I can easily send notes to let you and your parents know what is happening.

We might also be able to arrange for you to have some work to do! We can keep in touch with your parents about that. But whatever happens we won't forget that we are all part of this school, and we will still be working together as a school – even if it's not all in the same place *(adapt if necessary to meet your special circumstances)*.

Don't be too upset. We're all upset, but we know that we're all safe. We know that no harm is going to come to us. We have a problem, but it is a problem we can solve. There are some people who are going to help us who have dealt with this sort of thing many times, and they know exactly what to do.

Now, we might well find that some of your work has been damaged – things on the wall or in storerooms or on work surfaces. That's particularly upsetting – it makes me very angry, because I know how hard you all work, and you will probably be very sad after all the effort you put in. But work can be replaced. If we find that things have been damaged or lost, we will make new ones – I don't want you to worry about that. Please remember, that what's really important is that the real school – that's us, the people: the children, staff and parents – is safe and sound and ready to carry on as soon as possible.

One more word. Many of you, and your parents and many friends, may want to come in and help to clear up. At the moment, until we are clearer about what has happened and what is needed, we can't do anything. But I am most grateful for any offers, and when the time comes that we need help, then I will certainly let you know.

Before I tell you the arrangements for the rest of today, please listen quietly and carefully for a moment longer for this short **prayer/thought**.

☀ A prayer

Dear God, we thank you for our school, which is precious to all of us. Our building has been damaged, but we thank you that the people who make our school what it is are all still here, and so our school is still here, as strong and lively as ever.

We remember schools in the developing world – in Africa and in India – where many children have very little – a simple building, very few books, very little furniture. We feel a little closer to them today, and we thank you for showing us that where there is eagerness to learn and teach, then nothing else matters. Amen.

Serious damage to the school by fire, flood or vandalism

☀ A thought

Let's be thankful for our school, which is precious to all of us. Our building has been damaged, but the people who make our school what it is are all still here, and so our school is still here, as strong and lively as ever. We remember schools in the developing world – in Africa and in India. Where many children have very little – a simple building, very few books, very little furniture. We feel a little closer to them today, and we take to our hearts the lesson that where there is eagerness to learn and teach, then nothing else matters.

Pause.

☀ To end the assembly

Now to the arrangements for the rest of today.

Set out clearly the immediate arrangements you have made. Thank the school for being sensible and helpful and close the assembly.

© **pfp** 2002 ISBN 1 874050 57 0 May be photocopied for use only within the purchasing institution **pfp**, 61 Gray's Inn Road, London WC1X 8TH

Danger on a trip out of school

✦ Introduction

Every so often a school suffers from a traumatic event which affects a number of pupils directly and perhaps the whole school indirectly. Examples include a serious outbreak of food poisoning, a vehicle accident in which a number of children and perhaps staff are injured, or an accident or other stressful incident on a school journey. This assembly is intended for use in such situations. It is not for use when a death has occurred as a result of the incident. It requires some brief preparation – see 'Before the assembly' below.

Aims:

The aims of this assembly are to

- show the children that the school is responding to the event

- reassure the children not involved that they are safe

- reassure them that such events are rare.

✦ Background

When a school is directly involved in a traumatic incident, the effects can be profound. The school is likely to be of concern in the community at large and possibly the focus of media attention, and this will affect the children in a number of ways. Some may experience a sense of importance at being focused upon, and being involved in an event that is at the forefront of people's minds. Others may feel overwhelmed and confused at the situation. Those closely linked to the children directly affected may have a sense of anger and bewilderment. Many children are likely to feel emotional at some time in the few days immediately after the event.

The staff's and headteacher's role in this is to be calm and steady in their dealings with the children, and recognise that maintaining the normal routines of the school is the best way to help children come to terms with their feelings and worries.

✦ Before the assembly

Gather as many facts about the event as possible. You may not decide to use them all, but the more you know the better. Do not assume that either children or staff will know anything or everything, and remember that word of mouth retelling may well have distorted some of the news passing among them. If necessary, and if you have time, consult with any appropriate outside agency, such as medical services or police, to get accurate information.

Think also about the language you will use to present the information. Don't be reluctant to use appropriate language, although at the same time, avoid using aggressive or unnecessarily descriptive language which may upset or frighten children.

Note these details down – including any particular terminology that you have decided is appropriate – so that you have something to remind you.

Danger on a trip out of school

Meet with the staff before the assembly. Remember that they will be affected too and will need to talk. Use the meeting to let them know that you are going to talk about the incident in assembly, and to let them know the details as you know them, and any plans you already have for how the school will address the issue (for example, the terminology you have decided on).

Let them know that you will all meet again shortly, so that everyone can discuss, and agree, the common response that the school will take to the event.

● ● ● ● ● ● ● ● ● ● ●

The assembly gives you the option to suggest that children spend some time in the classroom doing things to provide help and support – if you choose to include this, make sure that you discuss it with the staff, too.

● ● ● ● ● ● ● ● ● ● ● ● ● ● ● ● ● ● ●

📖 The assembly

Make sure that when the children come in, they do so as quietly as possible.

Begin by giving as many facts about the event as possible, then simply and calmly continue as follows.

Every day, in every part of the world, there are sad and tragic happenings. There are accidents on the roads, in the home and at work, and illnesses, wars and famine.

But every so often, something happens that seems particularly tragic because it touches our lives and affects people we know and care for. That's what has happened to us, and as a school we have to come to terms with this and make sure we give all the support and thought we can to our friends who have been affected.

Events like these remind us that although life is very safe most of the time, dreadful things do happen.

Let's just take a moment to think about some of these things that are happening to people we know. After each of them, we'll just be quiet for a while so that we can think about them carefully.

Some of these points may need adapting slightly as appropriate to your situation.

Think especially of the children involved. We know they will recover and they will be back in school with us. Let's make sure we do all we can to help them. *Pause.*

● ● ● ● ● ● ● ● ● ● ●

Think of the families who are worried and concerned for their children. Let's all be as kind and helpful to them as we can be. *Pause.*

Think of all the people who have helped our friends already *(name any appropriate groups such as rescue services, police, ambulance people, hospital staff, doctors and nurses)*. Incidents happen every day which mean that people need them. In many cases things would be even worse if they were not there working hard for all of us. Let's be thankful for them, too. *Pause.*

● ● ● ● ● ● ● ● ● ●

And lastly, think of all the people out and about today who will return safely home. Think of your own homes, where you are safe. Let's be thankful for that. *Pause.*

● ● ● ● ● ● ● ● ● ●

Danger on a trip out of school

Now let's think what we can do. We can perhaps provide some words of comfort. Perhaps we could write letters, or make cards. Think about that in your classrooms after assembly. We'll need to try hard to find the right words to say, but if we do, I know our efforts will be very much appreciated.

☀ A prayer

Dear God, we are distressed today at what has happened to some of our friends. Help us all to be good and caring friends to them, and to be understanding and kind when they're back in school. Most of all let them feel your love and strength at this difficult time, so that they quickly recover from what has happened. Amen.

☀ A thought

After all that has happened, our thoughts are with the children from our school who have suffered. We, now, all have to be good and caring friends to them, and to be understanding and kind when they're back in school. Let's be grateful that we are all safe and well here in school and hope that everyone affected by what has happened will soon be able to feel as safe and secure as we do.

An act of violence against a child

✦ Introduction

This assembly is to use when a child in school has suffered severe or violent action such as abduction or physical assault at the hands of an adult. It is intended for use with the child's class or whole school depending on your circumstances and size of school – you may wish to change this to the whole year group. It requires some brief preparation – see 'Before the assembly' below.

Aims:

The aims of this assembly are to

- tell the children as much about what has happened as is possible

- dispel rumours as far as is possible

- remember the child and his or her family

- reassure the other children that they are safe.

✦ Background

In such circumstances many children will be feeling a whole range of emotions, including fear, sympathy and curiosity. Some are also likely to be very upset at what has happened to their friend. There will inevitably be rumour and wild conjecture about what has happened: the object of this assembly is to address this problem. It enables you to give the facts and to dispel the children's major worries as far as possible.

You need to be clear about exactly what you can tell the children, and about the language you can use. Be conservative about language. Avoid aggressive words such as 'stabbed', 'raped' or 'kidnapped', which have legal implications as well as being likely to frighten young children even more. You might instead use a phrase such as 'seriously hurt by a person who wanted to harm him or her'.

During the assembly the children will be quiet and apprehensive. They will look to you to seek reassurance from your facial expression and body language. Don't frown, for example, and if you have decided on a whole school or year group assembly, don't have whispered chats with colleagues while the children are coming in. Such actions will increase anxiety rather than provide reassurance. Smile and make eye contact with children and encourage colleagues to do the same.

✦ Before the assembly

If you are holding a whole school or year group assembly hold a brief meeting with your colleagues beforehand to discuss the approach you plan to take. Discuss the amount of information that you feel is appropriate to give the children. Let them know your policy on the use of language and that the purpose of the assembly is to provide calm and reassurance. Ask them, as suggested above, not to whisper to each other as the children come in, and to give

An act of violence against a child

careful attention to both their facial expression and body language.

You may wish to use music as the children enter to help provide an atmosphere of calm, for example, Satie's *Gymnopodie II* or Mozart's *Piano Concerto No. 21 – Andante*.

You may also wish to use the OHT provided on page 38 to provide a focus for the prayer at the end of the assembly.

Whether you are addressing the school, a year group or a class, write down exactly the information you have agreed is appropriate to give to the children. Note down

- where and when the incident happened, and any details of what happened

- the language and terminology you have agreed on

- the names of the child's family (they are mentioned in the assembly).

It's not an easy subject for you to address and notes will help you make sure that you say everything just as you have planned it.

📖 The assembly

Today we are all very concerned about *(name of child)*. You may know that something dreadful happened to **him/her**.

Give the details as agreed.

Now let's be quiet for a while and think.

Let's all think of *(name)*. **He/she** may be thinking about you all here, and wondering if you are thinking about **him/her** too, so let's make that come true. Each make your own picture of **him/her** in your mind. Perhaps you can picture a happy time you spent together – a time you have shared a joke perhaps, or solved a problem together in the classroom, or played a good game in the playground. Let's keep those pictures in our minds for a moment.

Pause.

And let's also think about *(name)*'s family *(name them)*. They will be worried and terribly upset at the moment. If you know them, make a picture of them in your mind. If you don't know them, then think for a moment of your own family, and how they might feel if someone in the family had been hurt.

Now, I want you to remember that an event like this doesn't happen often. But because of what has happened, over the next few days you might hear people talking about such things a little more than usual.

(Use the next sentence if appropriate.) You might also see reports about it on the local television news or in the local paper, perhaps. And sometimes, when something is talked about a lot, it makes it feel like it's something that happens all the time. In fact it is very rare, and I would like you to remember that. Most people will go through their whole lives without something like this happening, either to them or to someone they know. We know what we must do to keep ourselves safe. So we are safe in our homes and at school, and we each have our own individual places that we feel safe in, too.

An act of violence against a child

Now because many of us are upset, let's try to make ourselves feel a little bit better by thinking of those things and places that we know and feel comfortable in, and which help us to feel safe.

Where do you feel safe and comfortable? At home? Think of your homes for a moment, and the people there that look after you and care for you and keep you safe. Let yourself feel warm and comforted by the thought.

And how about school?

I hope you feel safe and comfortable at school too – we try hard to make it a place where you do feel that. Think of the places that are special to you in school – your place in class, your place in the cloakroom. Perhaps you have a favourite part of the playground, where you always like to sit or play. Let yourself feel warm and comforted by the thought of those safe places.

Now, just for a moment, let's put all those different thoughts together. Think of *(name)*, and **his/her** family, and think of all the special places that we have in our lives which help us to feel safe and warm and cared for.

When *(name)* is better **he/she** will come again to these special places and they – and the people in them, including us – will help **him/her** to put the terrible feelings behind **him/her**.

☀ A prayer

Dear God, help our friend *(name)* and all **his/her** family and friends at this sad and difficult time. Let **him/her** know that we are thinking of **him/her**. Help **him/her** to recover and once again to feel safe and secure, as we do in our homes and at school. Amen.

☀ A thought

We think today of *(name)*, our friend. Perhaps **he/she** knows that we are thinking of **him/her**, and wanting **him/her** to get better. We think also of **his/her** family. We know that they need lots of courage and strength at this difficult time.

(Name) found **him/herself** in a moment of danger. But let's remind ourselves that **he/she** has many good, comfortable and safe places just like we do – at home, at school, and with friends, family and people who love **him/her**. **He/she** will be able to find those special places again when **he/she** is better.

An act of violence against a child

Dear God,

Help our friend and all their family and friends at this sad and difficult time.

Let them know that we are thinking of them.

Help them to recover and once again to feel safe and secure, as we do in our homes and at school.

Amen.

An act of violence against a child

An act of violence against a child • OHT

Making fun of adults with special needs

✦ Introduction

Children making fun of adults with special needs can be both a common and upsetting problem. This assembly can be used in two ways – either as an immediate repsonse to an incident that has happened involving the children in your school, or as a general way of discussing adults with special needs in the community.

Aims:

The aims of this assembly are to

- help children see that making fun of others is unkind

- reassure children who have been upset by the taunting of the special needs adults

- give some facts about adults with special needs.

✦ Background

A group of adults with special needs in Warwickshire have made a video about their lives. One of the things that they all referred to was the problem they had with younger people and children making fun of them in the street. They were distressed by this and, quite understandably, genuinely unable to understand why anyone would want to do it.

In most communities, there will be adults with special needs, and sometimes they will be very well known. The taunting and, sometimes, even physical abuse that happens is often caused by older children. Although, of course, it is also possible that younger children are tormenting the special needs adults, and may well be in your school.

● ● ● ● ● ● ● ● ● ● ●

It is an issue that can be addressed in school in order to help both groups of children. For those children who aren't involved – particularly younger ones – seeing such aggressive and cruel behaviour can be very upsetting, and they are likely to be bewildered and confused. Those younger children who have participated in the taunting are often imitating older children, and have seldom thought through the effects of their actions. They may be embarrassed, or confused, and not know how to express these feelings appropriately. They may also be experiencing a sense of power over people who, in some ways, are less fortunate than themselves.

This assembly helps you provide reassurance to those children who have been upset by an incident, and to help promote better understanding.

✦ Before the assembly

If an adult who has been made fun of is a well-known member of your community, you may think it is appropriate to name him or her. If you do decide to do this, make sure you get their permission first. If they do give their permission, discuss with them any details you want to mention, so that you can be sure that your information is correct.

Making fun of adults with special needs

📖 The assembly

I want to tell you about Mark today. *(Be ready to say, 'No, not our Mark, another Mark!')*

Mark is twenty-four and lives at home with his mum and dad. He doesn't really have any real friends, although he does meet other people at a day centre that he goes to. He actually has real difficulty in making friends, because he's not very good at relationships with other people. Some people are like that. Just for some reason as one person has trouble with reading, or another has to struggle to learn maths, so there are some who find it hard to learn the skills of getting on with other people.

Almost all of us learn how to get on with others. We do it by watching people and understanding what they want and how they feel – you know if your friend is ready for a joke, or wants to tell you something. You know when you can join in a conversation and when you can't.

But Mark has not learned any of that. He just doesn't understand how it works, so he may well butt in and seem rude, or say something that is completely the wrong thing. And he won't understand if someone is upset, because he doesn't read the signs that they are, just as some people can't easily read the words on a page.

So Mark spends a lot of time on his own. He's happier that way. When he's with other people, they sometimes seem to get angry with him, and he's never really worked out why.

Mark has a special need, then. His special need, is to be understood – for people to understand that he does have difficulties in communicating. He wants to be able to go through his life without people getting angry with him, and telling him off for things that he can't help.

Mark doesn't go to work, because there aren't many jobs that he could do. Most jobs involve getting on with other people – listening carefully, trying to work out how they feel, being careful not to offend. And as we know, Mark has difficulties with all that. So he can't work and he has to depend on benefits. He doesn't like that.

However, there are other things he can do very well indeed. For example, he can play the piano and the organ beautifully. Nobody is really sure how he learned, because he's never been to proper lessons. The best guess is that he's just watched carefully at church and at concerts, because he's always liked going to church and to concerts. And he practises a lot at home and at church after the service.

It's amazing to see and hear him playing the organ, because you tend to think of him as just this strange chap with the very awkward manner and no ability to get on with anyone. Because he behaves strangely, people think he is stupid. But he isn't. You only have to see him playing the organ to see that. He has special needs alright, but he has special abilities, too.

Sometimes though, when he's out, people make fun of him, and shout after him in the street. He doesn't know why they do this. He really can't work out why anyone would want to do this. He is puzzled when they do it, and very upset. Why do they do it? He doesn't feel the need to call out after them. So why do they do it to him? *(Ask for ideas.)*

Making fun of adults with special needs

Now I've heard similar things about some of the people in this school.

I've heard that they have been making fun of somebody – calling **him/her** names and shouting after **him/her**. At first I couldn't think it was true – everybody here knows that we try to be kind and supportive.

Still, apparently it is true. Some people have been making fun of some people in our community who have special needs *(name the person, if you feel it is appropriate)*. I wonder why that is? Of all the people who pass by in the street, I wonder why it has to be **him/her** *(or use name again)* who is made fun of?

Adapt the following paragraph if you are talking about someone in particular.

Is it because they are different from other people? Well, perhaps they are. But then, I'm different from other people too, and so is everyone here. We all have different skills and abilities. We all have some things that we're good at, and other things that we're bad at.

• • • • • • • • • • • •

Do you know what is the most important and the most difficult thing that we all have to try to do in life?

Is it to climb a high mountain?

Or to run a great distance?

Or to rescue someone from drowning?

Or to pass a hard exam?

Optional *Take suggestions.*

It's not any of those. The most difficult thing is to accept other people for what they are. The great religions of the world have a lot to say about this. Jesus believed and taught that all human beings are worthy of love and

respect, and that the best rule of life is to behave to other people in the way that you wish they would behave to you. And when you look at other great religions – Hindu, Sikh, Buddhist, Islam – they say the same thing. Behave to other people as you would like them to behave to you.

And that means all people, not just some, and not just the ones you happen to like at the moment. Not just the ones who are like you. Not just the ones who are loving and cuddly to look at. Not just the ones who are the same colour as you. All human beings are equally worthy of respect and love and consideration. After all – that's the way you think of yourself isn't it?

In school, we try really hard to accept all of you and give you equal value. It isn't easy. We're all human. When someone misbehaves badly, we really have to work hard to remind ourselves that everyone is of equal value. We have to try to dislike the behaviour, and not the person who did it.

We can't start treating some of you differently because you look different, or because you walk differently, or because you can't do this lesson or that lesson. It wouldn't be fair would it? We try to treat everyone equally.

So I want you to try too – try not to judge people by their appearance or behaviour. Instead, try to imagine what it must be like for them. Every one of us has our own problems, our own difficulties and our own hopes and fears, and we can't tell what anyone else's are just by the way they look and behave. So it's important that we try to understand each person's problems, hopes and fears – just as we would want them to try to understand ours.

Let's finish with a **prayer/special thought** about that.

© **pfp** 2002 ISBN 1 874050 57 0 May be photocopied for use only within the purchasing institution **pfp**, 61 Gray's Inn Road, London WC1X 8TH
Making fun of adults with special needs • page 3 of 4

Making fun of adults with special needs

☀ **A prayer**

Dear God, we know that Jesus' message – and that of many other religions too – is simple to understand and difficult to carry out. That we should love one another as you have loved us, and as we want to be loved ourselves. Remind us of this constantly. Help us to treat all people with grace, compassion and respect. And help other people to treat us in the same way. Amen.

☀ **A thought**

If all human beings looked alike, and behaved the same, and could do the same things, the world would be a very dull place. And yet there's something inside some of us that makes us suspicious of anyone a bit different from ourselves. We have to overcome that. We must accept our differences, and try to understand each other. We must try to remember that everyone deserves love and respect, and remember to behave towards others in the way that we would like them to behave towards us.

© **pfp** 2002 ISBN 1 874050 57 0 May be photocopied for use only within the purchasing institution **pfp**, 61 Gray's Inn Road, London WC1X 8TH

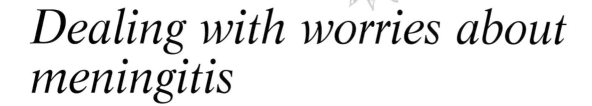

Dealing with worries about meningitis

✦ Introduction

Outbreaks of meningitis always raise the level of concern among parents, and children themselves may become anxious. This assembly gives some facts about meningitis that can be used to help children understand what the disease is, and provide some reassurance. It also gives some pointers to recognising the disease – spotting symptoms early is vital, and the national policy is to alert people of all ages to its importance.

Aims:

The aims of this assembly are to

- tell children what meningitis is

- provide a case study which shows that early action can result in a happy ending

- give a list of warning symptoms.

✦ Background

The suffix 'itis' on any medical condition means 'inflammation'. So meningitis is inflammation of the meninges – the lining surrounding the brain. There are two main kinds of meningitis – bacterial and viral. The bacterial form is the more serious. The problem is that it can rapidly give rise to septicaemia – blood poisoning – which is extremely dangerous not only in itself but because of the speed with which it can progress – a matter of hours in many cases.

Once septicaemia is established, it's a medical emergency of the highest order, and the patient often dies.

Tragically, young children under five seem to be among the groups susceptible to bacterial meningitis, so although it's extremely rare – there's about a one in one hundred thousand chance of getting it – the consequences are devastating enough to make it a genuine parental worry. That's why government and support groups are keen for people of all ages to know about meningitis and, especially, to be able to tell that someone has the disease.

✦ Before the Assembly

Talk to colleagues, and parent groups if possible, to judge their feelings about how you should do this assembly.

Use the OHT showing some of the symptoms –

Some of these might mean a child has meningitis.

- High temperature.

- Fever, possibly with cold hands and feet.

- Being sick or not wanting to eat.

- A high-pitched, unfamiliar cry.

- Blank, staring expression.

- Pale, blotchy complexion.

- Baby may be floppy.

- Baby may not want to be picked up.

© **pfp** 2002 ISBN 1 874050 57 0 May be photocopied for use only within the purchasing institution **pfp**, 61 Gray's Inn Road, London WC1X 8TH
Dealing with worries about meningitis • page 1 of 3

43

Dealing with worries about meningitis

- Baby may be difficult to wake.

- The soft spot on top of the head might bulge up.

- A blotchy rash.

These don't mean it's definitely meningitis – but always call a doctor or take the child to a doctor or hospital if you're even a bit unsure.

📖 The assembly

I know that some of you and your families have been talking about meningitis and perhaps worrying about it. So today I'm going to tell you some facts about meningitis and tell you a way in which you can help instead of just being worried.

Meningitis is an illness. There's more than one kind, some more serious than others. The serious kinds really are pretty serious. That's why people worry about it.

At the same time, it's very rare. Most of us adults have gone through life without ever knowing anyone who's had meningitis. We go for years without even thinking about it – and then there are some cases of people being ill with it, and it's in the paper and so we start thinking about it.

Here's a story about a baby who caught meningitis.

Little Donna was six months old when she started to be ill. She had a temperature and she was being sick a lot. She also had a rash. Even so her parents weren't too worried – babies do come out in spots and blotches

sometimes, and they thought she just had a bad cold or flu or something so they gave her some medicine and cuddled her to see if she would go to sleep.

However, Donna got worse. She seemed to be out of it – staring into space, and just whimpering a bit, and all limp in her dad's arms. They knew then that she must be pretty ill so they rushed her off in the car to the hospital. The doctors saw her straightaway and took her off for tests. When the doctor came back he said that Donna was very ill with meningitis and that it would be two days before they were sure she would be alright.

As you can imagine, Donna's parents were very worried, and they spent two whole days looking at Donna, and wondering if she was going to get better. The doctors and nurses worked very hard with her – she had her own nurse on duty with her all the time.

Donna had a severe form of meningitis, and she was very ill for some time before she eventually started to get better. Luckily her parents had taken her to the hospital in time and although she had a bad time, she did get better. And there weren't any after effects – that was lucky too, because children who recover from meningitis sometimes still have problems of some sort, such as deafness.

One of the problems with meningitis is that it's like flu or a cold at first – Donna's parents thought she had a bad cold. Then it starts to get worse, and by the time anyone starts to get really worried, the illness can have made quite a lot of progress. That's why it's a good idea to know some of the signs of meningitis. The more people who know these, the better – not just adults, but anyone who's old enough to spot them.

© **pfp** 2002 ISBN 1 874050 57 0 May be photocopied for use only within the purchasing institution **pfp**, 61 Gray's Inn Road, London WC1X 8TH

Dealing with worries about meningitis

So let me go through some of the signs of meningitis. You have to remember, though, that they may not all be there at the same time, and the person may never have all of them. If there's any doubt at all, the right thing to do is to call a doctor or get the person to the hospital.

If it's a baby, the signs to watch for are – high temperature, fever, possibly with cold hands and feet, vomiting or refusing feeds, high-pitched moaning, whimpering cry, blank, staring expression, pale, blotchy complexion, baby may be floppy, may dislike being handled, be fretful, difficult to wake. The soft spot on top of the head might bulge up.

If it's an adult or older child – high temperature, fever, being sick, diarrhoea, headache, stiff neck, joint pains, dislike of bright lights, drowsiness, fits, confusion. Both adults and children may have a rash.

Remember – there's no need to panic every time baby has a bit of a temperature. But if it goes on, and if there are other signs from the list, then it's probably time to do something – call a doctor, or an ambulance, or get someone to take baby to the hospital.

Don't go around being afraid of meningitis. It's very rare, and not all kinds of meningitis are really serious. But it makes you less afraid if you understand it, and if you know what to look for if you think someone may have it.

☀ A prayer

Dear God, help us always to give support and comfort to people who are ill. Help us to understand illnesses so that we are not afraid of them. Help us to use our knowledge to help people who need it. And be with all doctors and nurses who work with sick children. Amen.

☀ A thought

Being afraid comes of not knowing. If you're afraid of the dark it's because you can't see what might be there. If you're afraid of an illness it's because you don't know anything about it. But knowledge is strength – with some knowledge you can understand when you might be in danger and you can watch out for danger in other people.

Dealing with worries about meningitis

Some of these might mean a child has meningitis.

High temperature.

Fever, possibly with cold hands and feet.

Being sick or not wanting to eat.

A high-pitched, unfamiliar cry.

Blank, staring expression.

Pale, blotchy complexion.

Baby may be floppy.

Baby may not want to be picked up.

Baby may be difficult to wake.

The soft spot on top of the head might bulge up.

A blotchy rash.

An international crisis or the threat of war

✦ Introduction

This assembly is intended to reassure children at a time when the media is filled with news of conflict and fighting – a war or a threatened war such as the Afghanistan campaign, the continued conflicts in the Middle East, or the frequent images of violence in Northern Ireland. It requires some preparation – see 'Before the assembly' below.

Aims:

The aims of this assembly are to

- put some of the children's unspoken fears into words so that they can be shared and dealt with

- reassure children that a war or conflict does not directly threaten their homes

- pray for peace and for the safety of all people actually involved.

✦ Background

Many children harbour real fears when there is news of war and fighting. Television plays a large part in most children's lives, and on it they see a great deal of violence – both factual and fictional. When the same medium gives the impression that suddenly it is real and serious, they can become very fearful.

Remember that children are not able to place news of war in context in the way that experience enables adults to do, and they may think that their homes, parents and families are somehow threatened.

Also, remember that children, especially younger ones, do not easily distinguish fantasy and reality, so what is possible in fiction may seem to be possible in real life. A child who believes that Santa Claus will come bringing presents may also believe that evil people will arrive with bombs.

The tone of the assembly is deliberately calm and factual in order to provide the necessary reassurance, and to take into consideration what might be happening in children's homes – some families may well deliberately be keeping the worst of the war news from their children by rationing TV viewing. The assembly can't, of course, completely allay fears, but it will help (you may also want to do some follow-up work in classrooms).

In some cases, your school may have some children from armed services families who are perhaps more directly affected by relatives, or even their parents, being sent to areas of conflict. If this is so, then you should take advice from the families department at the base where the children come from, and from the parents of the children concerned. They are experienced in how to talk to children in these circumstances.

✦ Before the assembly

Make sure you have the basic facts of the situation clear in your own mind, and make a note of them to keep with you. Keep it factual – don't describe in graphic detail what has been

An international crisis or the threat of war

on the news, or adopt the media's often sensational or doom-laden approach. If there is anything which is uncertain, or mainly conjecture, then leave it out. You'll need to tailor the assembly to the kind of conflict. Clearly a continuing 'running sore' conflict like that between Israel and the Palestinians requires different language and emphasis from a major one-off war like that in the Falklands, the Gulf or Afghanistan.

📖 The assembly

I know some of you are worried about the way that there's a lot of fighting and conflict on the TV news at the moment. I'm sure you are aware that everyone is concerned about it – you may have heard your parents talking about it, for example. For the people involved it's a particularly worrying time, and in a while we will say a prayer/special thought for them.

I know that sometimes you worry about the war news too. You may think that enemies will somehow come into our town.

Well, I want to reassure you that that sort of thing won't happen.

The planes and the soldiers won't come here. The bombs won't drop here. Our lives here will go on as usual.

So when we see the pictures on TV, and when people talk about the fighting in a worried way, and when adults seem to be bothered about the war, it's not because they think that the fighting will come close.

Adults worry about the war because it affects our country in other ways – it costs both money and lives. Our soldiers, sailors and airmen and women might go off to fight, and it's likely that some people in the war zone will be injured and killed. Most of us find that a terrible thing to think about. Only a few wicked people really want to solve their problems by using guns, planes and ships and hurting others – most people would rather find other solutions. And most of us would like the money countries have to spend on war spent on helping each other rather than on attacking each other.

These are the reasons that adults worry, and they are the reasons why our politicians and leaders are working hard to bring fighting to an end very quickly. We must remember that at this very moment there are many people around the world trying to do just that – trying to find a peaceful answer to the problems that have caused this conflict. And it may be that they will find an answer soon, which means that peace will return in a very short time – that has happened before.

So you see, although everyone worries about a war, they are worried about the people in the war zone who will suffer.

We, too, can think about that. We can think about innocent people, including children, who are close to where there is fighting. For their sake, we pray for peace, in the hope that they will be able to be as safe in their homes and schools as we are today.

Let's have a **prayer/special thought** for the people who are affected, and **pray/hope** for the peace of the whole world.

An internatonial crisis or the threat of war

☀ A prayer

Dear God, we know it's a terrible thing that grown people cannot solve their problems without going to war. Be with the leaders on all sides of the trouble in *(name the war zone)* so that their minds will be concentrated on peace. Be with all the people out there who are directly affected – men and women on all sides who have left their homes to go and fight. Be with the families they have left behind and who will be worrying about them. Be with the people who live near the fighting whose homes may be affected.

We want a peaceful world for our children to grow up in – let that be the most important concern for all our leaders and politicians. Amen.

☀ A thought

We know it's a terrible thing that people cannot solve their problems without going to war. Let's hope that the leaders on all sides in the trouble in *(name the war zone)* will quickly find peace. And let's think for a minute about all the people out there who are directly affected. The men and women on all sides who have left their homes to go and fight. The families they have left behind and who will be worrying about them. The people who live near the fighting and whose homes may be affected.

We want a peaceful world for our children to grow up in – let that be the most important concern for all our leaders and politicians.

Preparing for a child using a wheelchair

✦ Introduction

This assembly is for a school that has, or is preparing for the arrival of, a child who will spend some or all of his or her time there in a wheelchair. It will help you accommodate the new pupil without fuss and without drawing too much attention to them. It requires some brief preparation – see 'Before the assembly' below.

Aims:

The aims of this assembly are to

• dispel some myths about wheelchair users

• help children see that everyone's surroundings are adapted to their particular physical needs

• help children towards having a balanced attitude to the newcomer.

✦ Background

The arrival of a physically disabled child in school will usually call for some preparation – often physical preparation of the building, and also some consideration of the attitudes and knowledge of the pupils and staff.

Younger children tend to be more tolerant of the different and unexpected. They will often be the ones who are curious but helpful. Older children may be keen (sometimes over-keen) to help, although some will almost certainly make unkind remarks, poke fun or even be aggressive. This is true for most schools – even those who think that unkindness or harsh treatment is not taking place.

It can be quite a difficult subject. There are issues which have to be addressed so that the child can be integrated as smoothly as possible, but also you need not to emphasise it so much that the child feels in the spotlight. This assembly helps you achieve this balance by taking a fairly lighthearted approach. It will help the pupils to consider, in practical terms, how they can resolve any conflicting feelings and attitudes they may have, and will provide guidance for them in ways they can help, exercise tactfulness, and make sure everyone is treated fairly.

✦ Before the assembly

You will need

• a ball to act as a 'glowing ball of gas', so preferably football-sized and orange if at all possible – at least a glowing colour.

and, if you choose to use the option

• an overhead projector

• a blank OHT

• the OHT provided on page 53.

Inform staff that you are going to give this assembly and that they may wish to do some follow-up work on attitudes to special needs.

Make sure you have all the facts about the child who will be joining you – for example, the type of wheelchair he or she will have and any other special need involved.

Also note down a list of all the work that is being done to adapt the school environment.

Preparing the school for a child using a wheelchair

📖 The assembly

Soon, a new child will be joining us here. Now I know that there's nothing particularly unusual in that, but this pupil is very special. **His/her** name is *(name)* and **he/she** will be bringing a wheelchair, because that's what **he/she** needs to get around.

Some of you may already know people who use wheelchairs, but some of you may not. So let me explain a little bit. Some people need wheelchairs because their legs don't work in the same way that ours do. Sometimes people in wheelchairs can't walk at all, and sometimes they can walk a bit, but need the wheelchair some of the time. *(Explain, if appropriate, which applies in this case.)*

Often they are called disabled, but let's not think of them like that. We go on legs, upright, they go on wheels, sitting down.

There are problems that people in wheelchairs have that we don't. Perhaps the main problem is that because most people go on legs, people on wheels keep coming up against obstacles that legs can cope with but wheels can't.

Can you think of some examples?

Take examples from the pupils – answers might include steps, rough ground, doorways, etc.

We haven't had a child in a wheelchair here before. The school is partly equipped to take them already. There's a ramp outside in case we have visitors in wheelchairs – or people with pushchairs – and the front doors are wide enough for chairs to get through *(name any thing else you already have in place)*. But we will have quite a lot more done because *(name)* isn't just a visitor. **He/she** will need to be able to get round the school to do an ordinary day, just like we do. So, we will have to make a few changes to the school – it will be adapted.

To adapt something means to make sure that it is built and arranged so that people can use it as easily as possible.

So, when you think about it, our school is already adapted for people who can walk on legs and run around and use their arms.

To help us think about that, let's suppose an alien came from outer space. Not a person at all, just a glowing ball of gas, sent to look at this strange planet called Earth. Suppose it looked at our school when no one was here. How would looking at the school help it work out what we look like? Would certain things about it tell it how we move around? Let's see.

Pick up the ball and use it as a character.

Here comes the alien. Ah ha!

What sort of place is this? A school? There's lots of things around that suggest that the creatures who spend time here work very hard learning things.

But what sort of creatures are they? How can we tell by the way the building is adapted?

Well, the doors have handles to push or pull, so they must have things on their bodies capable of doing that. The handles are all about the same distance above the ground, so their limbs must be about that height.

The doors are probably just high enough for the biggest of them to get through. But the doors are quite narrow, so these creatures must be taller than they are wide.

Look at the floors. How do the creatures get across them? They are level. Do they have wheels or do they walk? It might be wheels – but wait! Here are some steps. That seems to show that they must have limbs for walking rather than wheels.

Put the ball down.

Preparing the school for a child using a wheelchair

Let's leave our alien now, and think about what he's shown us.

Optional How else is school adapted for us?

Take some answers.

So – our school is built and adapted for a particular way of living. For people of a certain height, with two arms and hands, who walk. Even so, it's not convenient for everyone here. Can anyone tell me of anything in the building that's not easy for them?

Take some answers. For example, a small child may find the doors difficult to push open, or be unable to reach light switches or shelves or coat pegs. The floors may be slippery at times. Some steps on the playground may be steep.

Now let's think of people who are wheelchair users. They are people on wheels instead of on legs. Let's think again of our own building and what problems they might find.

Take suggestions.

Optional. *Write the suggestions on an OHT, or have one ready. Examples would be pushing doors open, reaching light switches, reaching coat pegs, negotiating steps, the toilets, the bumpy playground and a muddy school field.*

That's quite a few. And there will probably be lots more that we haven't thought of.

We may also need some new school rules. And that's something you can help with.

Think about some of our rules – no running in the corridor. How will that apply to a wheelchair user? Will we need a speed limit?

Suppose a wheelchair user persuades you to give a good push, and he or she goes too fast and bumps into someone. Whose fault is it?

We can't decide all these things now. We'll have to think about them with *(name)*.

Now let me show you these tips *(show the OHT)* for when you meet a wheelchair user.

- Don't say the person is 'disabled' or 'wheelchair bound'. Say 'wheelchair user'.

- Try to get to the same level when you talk – squat down or sit on a chair. Wheelchair users aren't keen on people talking down to them all the time.

- Don't touch or push the chair without permission. It's just like someone touching you or pushing you.

- Be ready to rearrange furniture so the person can get around the room.

- Don't be afraid to say 'Do you need any help?' but accept whatever answer you're given – don't push yourself on them.

- You can ask about the person's disability, but be polite and don't go on about it. They'll tell you what they want to tell you.

☀ A prayer

Dear God, please help us to understand some of the problems that different people have in getting around – problems that most of us take for granted. Help us to be welcoming and friendly to all who are in our school or who come to it whatever their needs, just as we ourselves were welcomed. Amen.

☀ A thought

We all take it for granted that we will be able to get around easily – whether we're at school, at home or going around the town. Let's think about some of the problems different people have to face in getting around, and let's try to be kind and thoughtful to all members of our school community, remembering their individual needs whatever they may be.

When you meet a wheelchair user

- Don't say the person is 'disabled' or 'wheelchair bound'. Say 'wheelchair user'.

- Try to get to the same level when you talk – squat down or sit on a chair. Wheelchair users aren't keen on people talking down to them all the time.

- Don't touch or push the chair without permission. It's just like someone touching you or pushing you.

- Be ready to rearrange furniture so the person can get around the room.

- Don't be afraid to say 'Do you need any help?' but accept whatever answer you're given – don't push yourself on them.

- You can ask about the person's disability, but be polite and don't go on about it. They'll tell you what they want to tell you.

Arrival and integration of an EBD child

✦ Introduction

The integration into mainstream of children with special needs can place pressure not only on teachers but on other children. Where the child being integrated has emotional and behavioural difficulties, there's a real challenge for teachers to draw something positive from what can be worrying or even frightening for all concerned.

Aims:

The aim of the assembly is to encourage and help children and families who are worried by the presence, arrival, or planned arrival of a child with emotional and behavioural problems.

(**Note** *It's important to read this assembly through and plan how to use it in your own particular circumstances. That may mean personalising it, or modifying it to suit your own school and children. The approach is what counts.*)

✦ Background

We can find ourselves using the term 'EBD' as an instant label, without analysing it. In fact, as the plural 'difficulties' implies, it actually covers a multitude of very different conditions. Fulton's *Special Education Digest* defines EBD as 'a range of difficulties including anxiety, phobia, obsessive/compulsive behaviour, withdrawal, depression, hypochondria, disruption, aggression, lack of co-operation, inattentiveness, delinquency (antisocial behaviour), bizarre thoughts and behaviour, lack of contact with reality, disorderliness of thought and action (psychotic behaviour)'. To that, we might add Attention Deficit and Hyperactivity Disorder (ADHD).

To read that list is to be alerted to one of the fundamental problems of this kind of labelling – we can all think of times and places when 'lack of co-operation' might be quite a good idea, and 'inattentiveness' could be an entirely appropriate response to some of our lessons. The danger, always, is of assuming that all children should shape themselves, or be shaped, to a predetermined notion of schooling. However the debate about integration develops, that's something for all of us to bear in mind all the time.

The integration of children with special needs makes extra demands on teachers and children, especially where a child displays behaviour that disrupts the class, or threatens or frightens other children. In good schools and authorities, there are agencies and individuals who give advice and support on curriculum content and teaching methods designed to help teachers to cope. It does help, though, if children begin to understand something about the child among them who behaves differently, or is 'naughty all the time'.

Arrival and integration of an EBD child

📖 The assembly

I want to talk to you today about behaviour. Nothing new in that you might think. I do talk to you about behaviour sometimes, don't I?

Yes, you're all nodding. But I'm not going to do any telling off today. The word behaviour, you know, really means all of the things we do – you know that, because there's good behaviour, there's sensible behaviour, there's courageous behaviour, there's frightening behaviour – I could go on for ages.

And all of those behaviours – the different ways we behave at different times – are controlled by what goes on inside our heads.

The big question, though, is how much we control what goes on inside our heads. That's a difficult one. To make it easier, let's listen to some stories about people – that's always the best way of making something a bit clearer.

• • • • • • • • • • • •

Here's Jamie, telling us about the day he got into trouble.

'Well, I was walking home from school with my sister, Tracy. I'd met her out of the infants, and I had to take care of her until we got home. As we were walking along, some big lads came running past and one of them knocked Tracy over. I turned straight round and grabbed the kid who knocked her over and pushed him into the wall. He banged his head on the wall, and I think he hurt himself – or I suppose it was me that hurt him. He didn't fight back or anything. He just walked away rubbing his head. Thinking about it, I was wrong to do that. He didn't intend to knock into Tracy, and in any case I should have looked after her instead of going for the

other boy. But something just made me do it. I lost control for a moment.'

• • • • • • • • • • • •

Now here's Julie, a grown-up remembering something that happened when she was ten.

'We used to go in this shop that sold sweets. An old lady kept it, and she would chat to us. We would talk to her and pretend to be friendly, but one of us would steal sweets while the others were talking to her. And as we went out she would say, "Bye bye, girls!" and we would say "Bye Bye!" back to her and then we would snigger and laugh outside the shop and share the sweets out. That was forty years ago, and I've felt bad about it ever since for all those years. She was a nice old lady who trusted us and we stole from her. What made us do it? What was going on inside us that made us do such a thing? If you know, please tell me, because I've wondered for all these years what it was.'

• • • • • • • • • • • •

Then there's Simon. He's fifteen and he's in a special unit for children who can't go to a mainstream school.

'I got excluded from school four times. I used to get into fights with other children, and I'd lose my temper and swear at the teachers, and once I threatened a dinner lady. I know I was badly behaved in class, too – I'd walk about and defy the teacher, and answer back and not do any work.

'And do you know, all the time I was doing it I knew it was wrong. It was as if there were two things going on inside me. People tried to find out – the educational psychologist came to see

Arrival and integration of an EBD child

me lots of times. One part of me was doing these things, and wanting to do them, and yet at the same time I wanted to stop and I was sort of crying inside even when I was sneering and laughing at people. I was so unhappy, and I know I was making my mum unhappy so that made me worse. People thought I was just a bad boy, but I was a very unhappy boy, really. I wanted someone to stop me doing these things, but when they tried to stop me I just got worse. It was terrible. Now I'm in a different place, and I think I'm doing a bit better. I hope so anyway.'

How do you feel about the people in these stories? Are you sorry for them? Or would you be hard on them and say they deserved to be punished?

I don't think there's an easy answer to that. Julie knew it was wrong to steal, didn't she? Jamie knew his first duty was to his sister. Simon knew that all of the things he did were wrong and made other people unhappy.

And yet – they all felt that something was making them do these things. How do you feel about that? I still don't think it's easy. If someone behaves badly, then they should expect to face the consequences, especially if they've hurt someone or made them unhappy. But at the same time, it's a good idea to try to see what's making them do bad things. Because it might be something they don't have a lot of control over.

Jamie? Well, Jamie just lost his temper. He reacted wrongly and he probably wouldn't do it again. If Jamie's mum had told Jamie off – really had a go at him, maybe taken his computer off him for a while, I think Jamie would have taken notice and done better next time.

Julie? I reckon she was led on by other girls. When you're in a crowd you do things that you probably wouldn't do on your own. She still shouldn't have done it though – she knew it was wrong. If her dad had found out he'd have gone mad at her, and she wouldn't have done it again.

And Simon? Not easy is it? Simon seems to have a real problem inside himself. It might be in his head, or he might never have learned the right things when he was growing up. Or he may just be a naughty boy who enjoys winding people up. Who knows? But if Simon's mum had told him off, would it have made a difference? Sadly, I don't think so. His mum is already upset about him. If his teachers told him off, would that make a difference? Maybe, for a while, but I don't think it would work for long. We know he's been excluded, and that must mean he's already been told off so many times that everybody's fed up of telling him off and that it didn't work.

Some boys and girls are like that – they just seem to go on annoying people no matter what anybody does. Does that mean we have to give up on them, and just let them stay at home annoying their families? I don't think so. We all have to keep trying. Teachers, dinner ladies, other people in the class. We all have to try. And it's not easy. But we don't give up. Teachers don't give up, parents don't give up, members of the class don't give up. It's a team effort.

Optional Jesus was very clear about this. Many times he told us to love the people who are difficult to love. It's something we must try to do.

Arrival and integration of an EBD child

A prayer

Dear God, please help us to understand some of the problems that different people have in getting around – problems that most of us take for granted. Help to be welcoming and friendly to all who are in our school or who come to it whatever their needs, just as we ourselves were welcomed. Amen.

A thought

We all take it for granted that we will be able to get around easily – whether we're at school, at home or going around the town. Let's think about some of the problems different people have to face in getting around, and let's try to be kind and thoughtful to all members of our school community, remembering their individual needs whatever they may be.

Traveller children in school

✦ Introduction

Children of traveller families may arrive in school, perhaps in significant numbers, quite unexpectedly. Other schools have travellers who are regular visitors or permanent communities.

In both cases there's a danger that the children will meet problems, the most common being abuse based on prejudice that often starts in the host community, whose collective opinion of travellers is usually low.

Aims:

The aims of the assembly are to

- emphasise the positive aspects of cultural and social diversity

- show that the choice of a travelling life is neither eccentric nor somehow wrong

- underline the school's commitment to welcoming newcomers.

✦ Background

In many ways, traveller families are pushed to the bottom of the heap. It's an old prejudice directed at gypsies, Irish travelling communities and, by association, anyone who chooses to live that sort of life. (It's not always realised that the Nazis put gypsies into concentration camps as well as Jews and homosexuals.)

This hostility manifests itself in various ways and shows in school life.

- Parents feel that traveller children are putting their own children at a disadvantage by taking up the teachers' time, or may slow the class down by behaving badly.

- There's straightforward racism, from name calling to violent behaviour.

- There's been evidence of subtle institutional racism – traveller children not included in school concerts, parties and so on.

- Some traveller children report being marginalized because of the assumption that they won't be staying – traveller children being 'left to draw at the back of the class' is an extreme example of this.

Each one of these is likely to be in direct conflict with your school's values. They will be dealt with in various ways – in PSHE, at parents' evening, in staff meetings and in group work with children.

Assembly adds a general statement of values about the acceptance of different ways of life.

It's important to realise that every local authority receives a grant for the education of the children of travellers. This normally supports specialist teachers, resources, classroom assistants and specialist welfare officers. The needs of travellers actually out on the road are catered for with distance learning packs and mobile units.

The authority's Traveller Education Service will always be the first point of contact when traveller families bring their children to school. They should respond quickly with information, support and resources.

Traveller children in school

Before that – even before travellers arrive – it's important that children are not drawn into casual condemnation of travellers, or into making quick judgements about their lifestyle. Before that again, therefore, it's important that teachers don't make the same quick judgments. Ofsted finds that the children of traveller families do best in schools 'which place great emphasis on equality of opportunity and, by encouraging the acceptance of ethnic diversity, establish an ethos which fosters self-esteem and pride in individual and group identity.'

Parents who are travellers are usually supportive of school at primary level, keen for children to learn the basics of literacy and numeracy. (It can be more problematic at secondary school, as the relevance of the curriculum becomes less obvious to travelling and fairground families. But even that sort of judgment may turn out to be the kind of instant cultural stereotyping that comes so easily.)

Knowledge about the traveller way of life, and about specific educational needs have to come from local authority specialists. There are many things to consider – the fact that children may be accustomed to staying with their family groups and could find it difficult to make relationships with others, the fact that they may be up late, and tired in school, the fact that they may wish to take responsibility for younger siblings in the same school. All of these, and more, can bring about unnecessary misunderstandings, and it's important to be armed with specialist knowledge.

✦ Before the assembly

If you're expecting travellers, or if families are newly arrived, arm yourself with facts – who they are, how many, what's known about the children. Your Traveller Education Service is the best source. Don't depend on hearsay. Share what you know with colleagues and outline the school's approach, for which this assembly will provide a lead.

📖 The assembly

Today we're going to think about people who live in houses or flats, and people who choose to live in caravans, either in one place or moving around.

Do you know anyone who lives in a caravan all the year round? Do you think that would be an exciting thing to do. Well let me tell you that sometimes it's exciting, but sometimes it's not. Let's hear from Ralph, who's lived in caravans all his life.

'I'm Ralph. I'm a traveller. We don't like to live in one place for a long time. We live in a place for a while and then we move on. There are lots of us around – you'll see our vehicles on the official sites, and sometimes parked by the roadside or on a bit of spare ground. We travel because our parents travelled, and they travelled because their parents did. I know my family were travellers before my grandfather's grandfather. A couple of hundred years ago they lived in simple shelters – like home-made tents in a way – that they could pack up and take with them.

Traveller children in school

Then a bit later, perhaps a hundred years ago, they started to use horse-drawn caravans. You'll have seen pictures of them – brightly painted four wheeled wagons with curved roofs and a good gentle horse plodding along at the front.

Then fifty years ago, my grandfather started off with a big modern caravan pulled by a truck. That's the sort of caravan I was born in, and it's the sort of caravan where I still live.

I'm proud of my caravan. It's got lots of bright chrome on the outside, and inside it's beautiful – my wife and I keep it spotlessly clean and we've got lots and lots of ornaments and china figures around. My mother was the same – visitors would wonder if we children ever knocked ornaments over, but we never did, and I trust my own children in the same way.

Not all travellers travel any more. That sounds strange, but it's very true. A lot of families live in caravans that don't move from where they are. And a lot also live in houses. How can you be a traveller and live in a house? Well, even in a house, travellers still feel part of the traveller community. And when you look in a traveller's house it'll remind you of my caravan – lots of ornaments and decoration, and perhaps some photographs and mementoes of the travelling life.

It's not always that they don't want to travel any more. Travellers come to a halt for various reasons. It may be because they want their children settled in school. It may be because it's got just too difficult to travel around. I know our group find it very difficult. You see

we really are supposed to use the official sites that the councils in the various towns provide for us – they have to provide a site by law. But sometimes the sites are full already. And sometimes – well, they're in not very nice places, on industrial estates, or in derelict areas. It's as if they really don't want us there, but they know they have to provide a site, so they just give us any old piece of land that's no good for anything else. They're not all like that, but some of them are.

Long ago it wasn't so difficult. Our grandparents and great grandparents could pull up their caravans by the roadside and let the horses graze there and nobody worried very much – and it was safe for the children to play. Now, though, the roads are busier, and it's dangerous to stop beside them – the police know that so they move us on. And if we go on to empty bits of land that aren't set aside for us, the landowner will get us moved on from there. And next time we come there'll be big boulders and earth barriers preventing us from getting into the land.

Everything's different you see. There's more traffic, there's not much land that's not needed, and somehow there doesn't seem to be room for people who want to live their lives moving around. I don't know about you, but I think that if some people want to move around with their homes instead of staying in one place, then they should be able to do it. It would be a pity if modern life didn't have room for travelling people. But it's getting like that, and I do wonder whether my own children will be able to carry on living as our family has lived for generations. Maybe they won't want to. I just hope they have the choice.

© **pfp** 2002 ISBN 1 874050 57 0 May be photocopied for use only within the purchasing institution **pfp**, 61 Gray's Inn Road, London WC1X 8TH

☀ A prayer

Lord, we are all your children. Help us to remember that, and to accept that people want to live in different ways, doing different things in their own way. May we be slow to judge people by how they look and what they do. May we be ready to learn from how other people live, and to enjoy the new experiences and new ideas that new people can bring to our school. Amen.

☀ A thought

As you go through life you often meet people who are very different from you – people with different interests, or from another country, or who live in a different sort of place – the countryside when you live in the town, or the city when you live in a village. When you meet someone like that, how do you react? The best way, I think, is to be interested, because you're going to learn something – about another way of life, another place, another way of looking at the world.

Same but different

✦ Introduction

Schools address themselves to issues of race and religion all the time, in a range of ways across the curriculum. In many places, good relations are under continuous pressure from outside – there are local community disputes, shadows cast by national events and opportunist threats to stability by groups seeking to profit from dissension and intolerance. This assembly can be used when there's any threat to the school's values on these issues.

Aims:

The aim of the assembly is to restate the school's stance on racial and religious tolerance.

✦ Background

Sadly, it's not possible to assume that school will always be a calm and tolerant place regardless of what happens outside. When there were terrorist attacks on the USA in 2001, for example, relations between Islamic and other groups came under pressure in many UK schools.

Local racial tensions surface, too, particularly in cities. For a long time, Asian communities have been targeted by racists – shops and homes vandalised, people, including women and children, abused in the street. The reaction of older members of these communities has always been to insist on using legal routes to justice – there's been faith that right would prevail. Increasingly, though, younger members are starting to question this and to fight back, with the result that we're starting to see street

fights and stand offs that occasionally degenerate into what the media are quick to label 'race riots'.

It's a hugely complicated picture, not least because of inner tensions in ethnic communities between different religious and racial groupings. And as if local pressures were not enough, there's a tendency for disputes which have their roots far away – in the Middle East, or on the Indian sub-continent – to reverberate in places like Bradford and Southall. And in rural areas, there are issues arising from infrequent contact with, and misunderstanding of other ethnic and religious groups.

It's difficult to avoid the conclusion – confirmed by many observers – that, in many communities, race and religious relations are getting worse rather than better. Teachers need to be aware, particularly, of reports from Northern Ireland which say that many community activities aimed at bridging the religious divide have actually exacerbated the problems, in that workers and children involved in mixed-faith organisations and projects have been abused and cold-shouldered by their own communities for doing so.

The lesson for schools is that although we can't ignore any of these issues, we can't be naïve about them, either. We can't solve the problems of centuries and we should take care before making quick judgments about motives and feelings. What we can do, though, is what we've

© **pfp** 2002 ISBN 1 874050 57 0 May be photocopied for use only within the purchasing institution **pfp**, 61 Gray's Inn Road, London WC1X 8TH

Same but different

always tried to do which is to affirm our own values in our own schools, having faith that we are acting as role models for what we know to be right. Our children will undoubtedly go their own ways when they leave us, but if we've managed to light a few small flames in a few hearts then we may be able to make a difference in the long term.

As always, the way forward is to look at the positive. So it's not a matter of saying that we're all the same really, but rather of celebrating diversity.

📖 The assembly

Are you a religious person? You know I think that's a difficult question to answer. Some of you would say 'yes' straightaway. Some would say 'definitely not'. And some would say they didn't know. And maybe some more would say that they really hadn't ever thought about it.

What is a religious person anyway? Do you think you know the answer to that? Put up your hand if you think you know the answer to the question, 'What is a religious person?'

(Take some answers. You may have answers that include belief in God, going to church or temple, saying prayers regularly.)

All of those are right, but I'm not sure they tell the complete story. I think religion means belief in something beyond yourself, that's better and everlasting and that gives you an example and some ideas to live up to. For example, Islam means belief in one God, and obedience to the prophet who is an example to others. And Islam has a holy book that sets out

what it is to be a Muslim. Good Muslims go to mosque, and observe the times of prayer and fasting, and they live life according to the rules set out in the holy book.

What about Sikhs? Do they believe in God? Of course they do. And they have leaders or Gurus who lived lives that show us how to live ours. There's a holy book, too, and a temple with times of prayer and celebration.

What about Christians? Do they believe in God? They do. And they have priests, and prophets and a holy book. And good Christians go to church.

I could go on – about Hindus, Jews and others. A religious person is someone who believes, has leaders or prophets to look up to, a holy book to live by.

So, are all religions the same as each other? Of course they're not. People believe in different things and worship in different ways. I only said a little bit about different religions – there's much more to say about them. Sometimes there are differences inside religions, too. There are different kinds of Muslims, different kinds of Jews, different kinds of Christians.

There's no problem about any of that. People aren't the same as each other, so it's not surprising that they worship in different ways.

Let me ask you another question. Do you think religious people should hate each other? Because sometimes it seems as if they do. On the TV you see people of different religions throwing bombs at each other and shooting bullets at each other. Should they be doing that? Of course they shouldn't. So far as I know, there isn't a single religion in the whole

Same but different

world that says you should hate people and throw bombs at them and shoot them. The people who do these things do them because they are human beings, with problems and difficulties that lead them to do things that they shouldn't do. We've all been in that position. We've all done things that we know we shouldn't do, because we couldn't see a better way. A starving person who steals a loaf of bread to feed her children is doing wrong, but maybe she can't see a better way. A religious person whose home and land is being attacked by someone from another religion may throw firebombs at his attackers because he can't see a better way. These things happen because we're human beings who aren't perfect. I'm going to read you a story that tries to tell you what I mean. This is a man called Michael, remembering his childhood.

When I was a boy I went to school in Birmingham. It was a good school. There were lots of different kinds of people there and I enjoyed that. There were people like me – Roman Catholics whose parents had come from Ireland to England to live and work. And there were Sikhs, and Muslims and Hindus and people from the Caribbean. We were different from each other, but in lots of ways we actually enjoyed being different. We didn't always mix together all the time, but so far as I can remember we didn't fall out or call each other names or anything like that.

Then something happened that changed that. One terrible night a bomb went off in a pub in Birmingham. Some people were killed and a lot of people were injured. It was the IRA that did it – Irish Republicans who were angry with the British Government. Now most Irish Republicans are Roman Catholics, and because

of that for a time there was a lot of anger against Irish Catholic families in Birmingham. My mother was shouted at in the street by people who were usually friendly with her. Our house had stones thrown at it, and my dad, who was a bus driver, had to stay off work for a bit and keep out of the local pub because there was so much hatred and anger about.

It was difficult for me at school, too. People of other religions – including Christians who weren't Catholics – wouldn't speak to me. Then one day I got into a big fight with some boys who had been calling me names and saying that my family must be murderers. Other Catholic boys joined in on my side and there was a huge fight on the playground at lunchtime.

Of course we were all in big trouble. I thought lots of us would be expelled or at least suspended. We had a tough head in our school – Mr Samuels – I suppose it was a tough school. We knew who was boss and we understood that it had to be like that. So we thought he'd come down on all of us like a ton of bricks.

But do you know what he did? He called a special assembly the morning after the fight, and he got me up on the stage. I remember most of what he said.

'This is Michael Donnelly standing up here with me,' he said. 'You all know him. He is Irish and a Catholic. Now I ask you this. Did Michael Donnelly blow up all those people in the pub the other night? Do any of you think he did? Did Michael do any of the other things that have happened in Northern Ireland? No? Then why are you blaming him for them? That doesn't make sense to me. And you are all sensible people so I don't understand why it makes sense to you.'

© pfp 2002 ISBN 1 874050 57 0 May be photocopied for use only within the purchasing institution **pfp**, 61 Gray's Inn Road, London WC1X 8TH

Same but different

Then he said, 'You know me, too. I am Mr Samuels. I am a Jew. I came here from Poland when I was a child. I am the only one of my family left. My parents and my uncles and aunts and my older brothers were murdered by the Germans in the time of the Nazis. The Nazis thought we were an inferior race. That means they thought we weren't really human beings at all, and could just be killed.'

Mr Samuels stopped and looked at us. We were completely silent. He had never told us this before, and we were shocked. Then he went on.

'Over there among you is John Muller. His parents are German. They came here because Mr Muller's work brought him here. Should I hate John? Should I hate his parents? Did the Mullers murder my family? What would you think of me if I refused to teach John, or if I called him names?'

He looked at us again, not speaking, and we just stood silently thinking about what he had said.

Then he said, 'All over the world, Jews and Muslims argue with each other. Sikhs and Hindus fight each other. Protestants and Catholics fight each other. They do that because sometimes their feelings get the better of them. We try to understand that, but we don't have to think it's right. Here in school there should be no hatred between us. We enjoy all the different people we have here. Look at our school photographs on the walls and in our brochure. We're all colours, all shapes and sizes, and do you know what? Everyone's laughing. "Look at us!" we're saying. "We're all different, but we like it like this. Why don't you come and join us!"'

After that we still had the occasional bit of bad temper, but there were no more bad fights, and we all made an effort to get on together. I only wish the rest of the world had been able to hear what Mr Samuels said that day.

☀ A prayer

Lord, help us to understand and respect all our fellow human beings, because we know that you love all of us, and that you do not want us to fight among ourselves. May we be slow to be angry, and quick to forgive. Amen.

☀ A thought

Do you blame a person for something done by someone else in another place? Of course not. And yet that's what seems to be happening in so many parts of the world. Let's try not to put labels on each other too quickly – Jew, Muslim, Hindu, Sikh. We're people first, and the label comes after.

Refugees – unexpected new arrivals

✦ Introduction

Many schools find themselves accepting sudden new arrivals, such as refugees. This assembly requires some brief preparation – see 'Before the assembly' below.

Aims:

The aims of this assembly are to

- remind pupils of the need to welcome strangers

- reassure pupils that the school is a place where all children can work and grow together

- make explicit the school's values of tolerance and fairness.

✦ Background

The sudden arrival of children from a different culture or country can be disturbing for parents and children, and prejudices can surface. Children from a very different culture from our own are likely to behave in ways that appear strange to other pupils in the school. This can cause some children to react in a hostile or power-seeking way, which can upset and confuse not only the new arrivals, but others in their peer group. Some children may feel threatened by the very presence of the new and, to them, strange pupils. Others may feel neglected if, or when, special attention and care is shown by staff to the new arrivals. Perhaps the best predictor of those who may be likely to

feel resentful is the child's own status within his or her class at the time the new children arrive.

At this time, a school has to reassert its values of tolerance, openness and justice. Much of the work will go on in class, but an assembly is helpful. Although there is sometimes little warning in such a situation, the assembly is intended for use before refugees from other countries are due to arrive.

✦ Before the assembly

Make information lists about the new arrivals including their names, country of origin, their language and reasons for leaving their country.

Prepare a map, preferably on an OHT, which shows the country they are coming from.

Optional Also prepare an OHT map of Northern Europe which clearly shows the Channel Islands.

📖 The Assembly

Very soon we will be having some new children join us here in school. Now that's not unusual – we often have new children coming to us during term time. But these children are different in some ways and they'll need your help to settle in. Let me tell you something about them.

Give the facts about the new arrivals – explain how many there will be, where they are coming from and perhaps some background as to their reasons for leaving their home country.

Refugees – unexpected new arrivals

So when our new arrivals get here they will be feeling that our **city/town/village** is a very strange place.

Now, you know the story of when Jesus was born. His mother and father were in a strange town, with nowhere to stay. They knocked on doors, and could not find anywhere to go. They were really anxious because Mary, the mother of Jesus, was very near to having her baby.

You know the story. An innkeeper took Mary and Joseph in, and gave them room in a stable. And there the baby Jesus was born.

All through His life on Earth, Jesus emphasised the need to be welcoming to people who come asking for help or shelter or food. Many Christians take this message to heart. The Salvation Army has hostels, and many Christian groups go out into city streets at night, to give food and comfort to people who are sleeping rough because they have no home.

Other religions do the same. Every Sikh temple has a kitchen and will give food to people who call in and ask. Sikhs believe strongly that people are equal and that everyone should be welcomed and helped.

Do we keep these traditions and customs, do you think, here in school?

Do we always welcome newcomers who turn up? Do we welcome people who come to our country, or to our town? Usually we do. But, just occasionally, someone is thoughtless, usually because they are afraid of the newcomers, or don't understand their ways.

When our newcomers arrive, there is no need for any of us to let that happen. When they arrive I want all of you to show them kindness and understanding. Those are things our school believes in.

Listen to this story.

'Gran,' said Steven. 'We've got these new kids in our class.'

His gran wiped her hands on the tea towel and turned away from the sink. 'Oh, yes? Who are they, Steve?'

'They're from somewhere in the Middle East. Not sure where exactly. They don't speak a word of English, either. I don't think it's fair.'

'What?' said his gran. 'You mean it's not fair that they don't speak English? French people don't speak English. Is that unfair too?'

She laughed and Steven laughed with her. 'No. I mean they take up a lot of the teacher's time. And the class has suddenly got very big. There's hardly room for them. And I think at least one of them is too old and ought to be in the high school.'

'Are they happy?' asked his gran.

Steven stared at her. It wasn't the question he was expecting.

'Well?' went on his gran. 'The biggest thing I worry about with you, is whether you are happy. So that's the most important thing for them. Are they happy or not?'

'Well, I don't know,' said Steven. 'One of them cries a lot.'

'Think about it, Steve,' said his gran. 'I expect they've been having a very difficult time in their own country – the place that they feel at home and comfortable in, like you do here. In fact, it's got so bad that they've had to leave their homes, and probably most of their families, and come to a strange country where they don't know the language. And what they find is whingeing Steve, saying they take up too much of the teacher's time. Isn't your

© pfp 2002 ISBN 1 874050 57 0 May be photocopied for use only within the purchasing institution **pfp**, 61 Gray's Inn Road, London WC1X 8TH

Refugees – unexpected new arrivals

teacher always on about being kind and understanding?'

'Yes, but...' said Steven.

'No buts!' Gran said quickly. 'You're either kind and understanding or you're not. It's easy enough to be kind to someone who doesn't make demands on you – you can be kind to a smiley baby, or a good friend. The real test is being kind to someone who is feeling really down, who you don't know very well and who needs a lot of attention. Now, let me tell you something. Have I always lived round here?'

'No,' said Steven. 'You came from Guernsey during the war. You've told us. We went there on holiday to see your old home once.'

'I need to remind you again, obviously.' Gran smiled and nodded to the dresser. 'Let's get the map out.'

Optional *Show the OHT of Northern Europe with the Channel Isles clearly visible.*

She pointed to a small spot off the south coast of England. 'Here's Guernsey. It's one of the Channel Islands, but part of Britain. Here are the others – Jersey is the biggest. Where's the nearest mainland?'

'France, here,' Steven pointed to France, just below the islands.

'That's it,' said Gran. 'So when the Germans conquered France during the war, we were obviously going to be next. So a lot of children and families left before that happened. We came here. Can you imagine what it was like?

'I was ten. I had spent all my life on a beautiful island with my parents who were farmers. It was quiet and peaceful there, and we all knew each other. It was a lovely community. And then I found myself in this big town. I had never seen anything like it. I didn't even

understand the language – we did speak English in Guernsey, but we also had our own language that we spoke a lot at home, and I really couldn't understand the way English was spoken here. Everyone talked so quickly and in a strange accent.

'At school, people were cruel to me. They made fun of the way I spoke. They made fun of my clothes. They treated me like an outsider. The teachers didn't protect me much either, because I think they thought I was an outsider too. Luckily, today's teachers are a bit better informed about the outside world. Only one person was really kind to me – a little boy who gave me an apple from his garden one day. That cheered me up and I've always remembered it.'

'But you settled down,' said Steven.

'Yes, I never went back. But it was a hard struggle, and it would have been so much easier if a few people had said a kind word to me. So don't you talk to me about it not being fair when someone comes into class who needs some attention. You go to school tomorrow and be kind to your newcomers. They might not know the language, but they understand a smile, and the offer of a crisp out of your bag. You just remember your gran all those years ago. I tell you, if I hear of any trouble, I'll be down there to remind them what it's like.'

'You could come and talk in assembly!' said Steven.

'I might very well do that,' said his gran.

Pause.

Look around our school. Look at the names of our pupils and our adults. They remind us that in our country we have many families who originally come from somewhere else – from Ireland, Belgium, Scandinavia, Africa, Jamaica,

© pfp 2002 ISBN 1 874050 57 0 May be photocopied for use only within the purchasing institution **pfp**, 61 Gray's Inn Road, London WC1X 8TH

Refugees – unexpected new arrivals

India, Pakistan, Malaysia, Hong Kong. Somewhere in the history of each of these families there is an arrival in a new country. And a person who was longing for understanding and a kind word or gesture.

So when our new people come into our school, let's remember that what counts is kindness and understanding. Things might be difficult at first as we all get to know each other, and get used to each other's ways. But that's no different from meeting anyone new – and all those problems can be overcome as long as we make a little effort.

☀ A prayer

Dear God, we know that you want us to welcome strangers. The story of Jesus is the story of a man whose parents were refugees who could find nowhere to stay. Each year in our nativity play, we act out the story, and we remember the innkeeper who found room for Mary and Joseph in a stable. Help us to remember that kindness to strangers is a basic principle of life. Help us to welcome all newcomers to our school and to make them part of our community. Amen.

☀ A thought

All of us arrived in the world crying and a little afraid. But we were immediately comforted and loved. Each time we go home, feeling down and unhappy, we are given love and support. If ever we have to go to a strange place, among new people, then we hope to find some of that love and understanding there. So when we are in a position to give comfort and kindness and love to people who need it, let's make sure we remember and are ready.

Refugees – unexpected new arrivals • page 4 of 4

69

The closure of a major local employer

✦ Introduction

This assembly is intended to be one element in the school's endeavour to support children and their families during the period when a major local employer is making large numbers of employees redundant or is undergoing total closure. It requires some brief preparation – see 'Before the assembly' below.

Aims:

The aims of this assembly are to

- give support to children and their families

- try to dispel some of the children's main concerns

- to present the facts of the situation.

✦ Background

The sudden closure of a major employer can be devastating to a community. It will be talked about in most households, even those not directly affected. Most parents will try hard not to reveal their worries to their children, but the concern will inevitably come through. The children may well overhear conversations about money and mortgages and loan repayments, and they will probably see press and television reports. The effect of all this on a child is often to make things – bad as they are – seem even worse. Children may harbour thoughts of being homeless and penniless, or of the family somehow being split up.

The school cannot pretend to address all these fears. However, it can provide continuity and stability, and provide reassurance about the ultimate survival of the community and the family. Parents usually want the school to fill this role for their children at times like these.

In dealing with such an issue, however, it's very important that the tone you use is right. This assembly is designed to help you achieve that. Its approach is to be factual and reassuring – not falsely and unrealistically reassuring, but simply reminding the children that family and community ties are very strong, and that setbacks are often followed by regeneration.

This will, of course, be only one part of the action you take as a school, but support beyond this is best given through individual counselling or quiet talks in class.

There are two related traps for headteachers and teachers to avoid, throughout all dealings with the children and their families. First, don't be preachily bright and breezy. 'Always look on the bright side of life' isn't appropriate for families in crisis.

Second, don't forget that teachers with relatively well-paid permanent jobs have to be very careful how they counsel people affected by unemployment and financial difficulty.

The closure of a major local employer

✦ Before the assembly

Make sure that you have the facts. If necessary delay the assembly half a day to give you time either to see or phone the employer's representative yourself. It may be possible to meet with other headteachers in the area so that you can visit the employer together.

It's possible that the employers will be reluctant to find time to meet with you in what will inevitably be a busy time for them. If this is the case, explain that as headteacher of the school to which their employees' children go, you feel you have the right to be told by them what the position is. A powerful argument is to point out that this would be far better than you depending on press reports.

Once you have done this, gather the staff for a brief meeting before the assembly. Tell them

- the facts as you know them

- the philosophy of the assembly – that it will be factual, and quietly and modestly reassuring

- remind staff of the traps they need to avoid as they talk to children and families.

📖 The assembly

I know that you have all heard of the **closure/problem** at *(name the company or organisation)*. A lot of people in our community are worried about this, because if the place where they work closes, then they may well end up without a job.

Having a job is important to most people. It makes them feel wanted – if you drive a bus, or teach in a school, or deliver the post, or put engines into cars, or design or build houses, you know that you're doing something that

other people depend on. You have to do your job correctly. And doing that makes you feel wanted, and makes you feel good about yourself. Even if the job is not all that pleasant or exciting, and even when there are bad days, it can still make you feel wanted. If you didn't turn up one day, someone would ring you up and say, 'Hey, where are you? Get down here, we need you.'

So somebody whose job is suddenly taken away from them can feel unwanted. One day you are needed to drive that bus or deliver the post, and the next day nobody wants you to do it. So you stay at home and nobody rings you up and says, 'Hey get down here'. It's as if they have suddenly forgotten all about you.

When you go to work, you get into a routine, too. You have friends there, you have your locker or your desk, you have your own coffee mug hanging up. It's not as homely as home, but it is a kind of place of your own all the same. A bit like school, where you come in, hang your coat on your own peg, meet your friends, go to your own place in class. If school wasn't there all of a sudden you'd miss all that. And for an adult, if your work disappears you miss all that too.

So losing a job can make people feel unwanted and unhappy.

Of course, the other big worry that people have when they lose their job is about money. People go to work to earn money to buy food and clothes for themselves and their families and to pay for their houses. If they have no job, the amount of money they get becomes less, and so they have to think very carefully how they are going to manage to pay for all those things.

The closure of a major local employer

Now some of these things are happening in our own community at the moment. *(Name the company or organisation)* is going to **close down/lose lots of staff** and quite a lot of people who work there will lose their jobs. So these people are going to worry about not feeling wanted, and they are going to worry about not having as much money coming into their home.

Perhaps the people in your homes are worrying about this. Even if they are not directly affected, they will be concerned about the general effect on the community. I won't pretend that it isn't serious, or that there's nothing really to worry about, but I will say one or two things that I hope will help you, and reassure you.

You have a part to play in helping your families. If people are feeling worried and uncertain and unwanted – your mum or dad, or grandparents, or brothers or sisters perhaps – then you can let them know that you still want them, and that they are still very important to you. You don't have to go over the top, but just be thoughtful and understanding. Don't make extra problems at home, bring a smile into the house when you can, and make sure your family know that you love them.

Remember that whatever happens the love in your family is stronger than anything else. A mum or dad, or a step-parent or a grandparent or an older brother and sister who loses his or her job, is still the same person as before. They may seem a little different, because they might be more miserable and quiet and thoughtful and worried than usual, but each one is really just the same person you knew before.

Remember, as well, that although people worry about paying the rent and paying the mortgage, they can usually sort things out. When people lose their jobs they lose their wages. But that doesn't mean there's no money at all. There is money from the government to help people over their difficulties. There's less money than before, certainly, and everybody in the house – including you children – has to think of having less to spend. But there is some money.

At a time like this, help your family and friends in our community. Come to school so that your families have time in the day to think about how they can sort things out. Don't take more problems home than necessary – do your work, keep out of trouble. Make sure you play your part in keeping love and thoughtfulness alive in the home. Eventually, we hope that things will start to look better. In some places where this has happened, other employers have moved in and there have been new jobs. I won't say this is definitely going to happen, and it always takes time – but that is something that we can all hope for.

The closure of a major local employer

☀ A prayer

Dear God, our community is in some trouble at the moment. Help us to help our families at this difficult time. As Jesus said, it's our duty to love one another. Help us not to be too sad, but to keep looking forward and try to keep on top of our problems. Also help us to find new opportunities at this difficult time. Amen.

☀ A thought

Our community is in some trouble at the moment. Help us to help our families at this difficult time. Let's remember our duty to love one another. Let's not be too sad, but keep looking forward and try to keep on top of our problems. Let's hope our friends and families can find new opportunities.

© **pfp** 2002 ISBN 1 874050 57 0 May be photocopied for use only within the purchasing institution **pfp**, 61 Gray's Inn Road, London WC1X 8TH
The closure of a major local employer • page 4 of 4

Smoking

✦ Introduction

This is an anti-smoking assembly. It can be used at any time, but may be particularly useful if there's concern about particular children being caught smoking, or if it's clear that pupils are smoking outside school.

Aims:

The aims of this assembly are to

- show children the dangers of smoking

- show children that refusal to smoke is a good decision

- help children worried about adult smokers in their homes.

✦ Background

Imagine a roomful of teenage smokers (and it wouldn't be too difficult to find them). How many of them will die from smoking (assuming they don't give up the habit)? The answer is that half of them will be killed by their habit, and, of those, half will die while still in middle age.

The relevance for parents and teachers is that adult smokers are typically captured between the ages of eleven and fourteen – 70 per cent of adult smokers started then – and there's plenty of evidence that children try smoking at primary school age, right down to the age of five.

Smoking is implicated in a huge number of conditions from cancer and strokes to bad breath. It's increasingly realised, too, that passive smoking has a significant effect. Some 17 000 children under five are admitted to hospital with conditions attributed to sharing a home with smokers.

Clearly, the major responsibility in this is for parents. Schools, though, should be involved. Apart from warning children about the dangers of smoking, teachers can give support to the many children who worry about parents and grandparents who smoke.

Most schools will work on this in science and in PSHE. The assembly provides support for that classroom work.

✦ Before the assembly

You need the OHT that sets out some of the facts.

📖 The assembly

Today we're going to talk about smoking. I reckon some of you have had a go at smoking. Having a go at it is quite natural really – maybe we all tried it to see what it was like. But making it into habit is a very bad idea. Why? Because taking nicotine and smoke inside your body is bad for your body. It's as simple as that. You want to know why smoking's bad? Look at the OHT.

I'll start with a story.

Once upon a time there was a little girl called Rosie. Now Rosie was a bright and breezy sort of girl, ready to try anything. And not surprisingly when she was about eight she had a try at smoking. She found some of her dad's cigarettes and matches on the mantelpiece at home while her parents were out, and so she lit up. And what do you think happened? Why, she was horribly sick because the tobacco smoke and the nicotine didn't do her any good at all.

You'd think, wouldn't you, that an experience like that would put her off? After all, feeling sick is a pretty good sign that your body is trying to get rid of something that it doesn't like, or that might do you harm.

But no, Rosie wasn't put off at all. She tried one of her dad's cigarettes quite a few more times after that. She wasn't sick again, and eventually she managed to convince herself that she quite liked smoking after all.

Then when she was eleven she started smoking seriously. What happened was that she made friends with some older girls she met down at the recreation ground. They were regular smokers, and they'd say, 'Come on, Rosie, have a fag.'

Rosie felt quite grown up standing around with the girls with a cigarette in her hand.

The problem, though, was money. She couldn't keep taking cigarettes off the other girls, and she only had a small amount of pocket money. As a result, she seemed never to have any spare pocket money for sweets, or for going to see a film or anything. She was always borrowing off her mum.

So when Rosie became a teenager she got a Saturday job. Even so, she seemed to be spending a lot of her money on cigarettes. So she decided that she wouldn't smoke any more. But the trouble was that she couldn't give up. Smoking, you see, is addictive. That means once you've started it's really difficult to give up. You actually feel bad if you try to give up. So Rosie kept on smoking.

Then Rosie got a boyfriend. She liked him very much. But before long he gave her up. She didn't know why until one of her friends told her. It seems her ex boyfriend had told her that Rosie smelled too much of cigarettes – her clothes smelled of tobacco, and her breath wasn't too pleasant, either.

Rosie was upset by that, so she decided again to stop smoking. But again she failed. She felt terrible and she was soon tempted back. For one thing she had too many friends who smoked.

Eventually, Rosie found a boyfriend who smoked too, and as time went on they got married and moved into a small flat. If they'd added up how much money they spent every week on cigarettes, they would have realised that they could have afforded a bigger flat, but somehow they never seemed to work that out. What they did work out, though, was that Rosie's sister wouldn't come and visit them very often because she said the flat smelled of cigarettes. And when Rosie's sister had a baby she stopped coming altogether, because she said she wouldn't bring the baby into a place where people smoke.

Rosie and her husband tried many times to give up smoking. In fact, it became a bit of a joke between them and among their friends. On the first of January everyone would say, 'What's the New Year Resolution this year, Rosie? Don't tell us, we know already!' And everyone would laugh. Rosie would join in the laughter, but inside she was really upset that she couldn't give up.

Rosie smoked all her life. She never succeeded in giving up. As she grew older she had lots of things wrong with her that were caused by smoking – she was short of breath, and she was coughing all the time. And in the end her life was much shorter and less pleasant than it

Smoking

could have been. All because when she was a lively little girl she tried something new. At the time, it seemed to be a good idea – quite a laugh really – but it ended up capturing her and not letting her go. And it spoiled quite a bit of her life for her.

• • • • • • • • • • •

A lot of people have a try at smoking. Some keep on doing it until they like it. And that's where the problems start, because once you like it, it becomes really difficult to give up. You think you can, but you find you can't. You lose the freedom of choice. Why is that? It's because regular smoking makes invisible changes in your body. If you stop smoking then, your body notices that you've stopped and it needs to change back to how it was. But changing back is difficult and painful and you feel terrible while it's happening. It's just easier somehow to carry on smoking. If you carry on smoking you carry on with other things.

You carry on having smelly clothes.

You carry on damaging your lungs.

You carry on having bad breath.

You carry on spending money that's going to go up in smoke.

You carry on upsetting other people with your smoke.

You want to stop doing these unpleasant things. But it's too late. You can't stop.

• • • • • • • • • • •

Let me ask you this. Is someone in your house trying to give up smoking? Or thinking about giving up? Then what can you do to help?

Surely you'd like to help them to stop doing something that's harmful to them?

• • • • • • • • • •

How can you help? Here are some ideas.

Keep giving encouragement – 'Well done! We're on your side!'

Make a chart to put on the wall – how many smoke-free days.

Give rewards – a hug or a cuddle is probably as good as anything else you could offer.

Say how much better the person is looking.

Say how much more pleasant the house is without smoke.

• • • • • • • • • •

Can you think of any more?

☀ A prayer

Help us to take care of our bodies, Lord, and to keep away from things that will harm us or make us ill. Give us the strength to help other people who want to live more healthy lives.

☀ A thought

You get a little paper tube, fill it with dried vegetation, then you set fire to it and suck the smoke in. Ridiculous, isn't it? Even if the little tubes were free it wouldn't be very sensible. So how sensible is it to pay good money for them?

Smoking is bad because –

It damages your lungs.

It can cause cancer.

It can cause other illnesses.

It makes your breath smell.

It makes your clothes smell.

It affects other people.

It costs money you need for other things.

I don't want to go to school (bullying)

✦ Introduction

This assembly is to use either when there's been concern about particular incidents of bullying or to reinforce the school's bullying policy.

The assembly requires some brief preparation.

Aims:

The aims of this assembly are to

- demonstrate that the school takes bullying seriously

- reassure children afraid of bullying that they can speak up

- reassure bullying victims that they are not to blame.

✦ Background

If there has been a bullying incident, or a series of incidents, they will have been dealt with individually as part of the school's behaviour policy. There comes a point, though, where the school's attitude has to be stated publicly in assembly. The idea of this assembly is to help you to do just that – both to reassure children who may be afraid and to let the whole community know that such behaviour will not be tolerated.

An important theme in all bullying policies is that the victim is not to blame. It's important to recognise this, because it's very easy for effort to be diverted away from the problem itself and

towards getting victims to behave differently – to "ignore it" or to "be assertive". There's obviously a case for improving the self esteem of children who are bullied, but the priority always should be to assert each child's right to be the person he or she is, in safety, protected by adults. The school's first priority, in other words, is not to focus on the victim but to stop the bullying.

This assembly strongly reinforces that view.

✦ Before the assembly

You will need

- the OHT masters supplied on pages 82–83

- an OHP

- an A4 sheet of paper to mask some of the text.

Inform staff that you are going to give an assembly on bullying.

📖 The assembly

We all know what bullying is. Shall we put it into words?

(Uncover each line of OHT 1 in turn, until the end of the first section.)

A bully is a person –

Who teases or name calls someone to make them upset.

Who deliberately picks on people who will be upset.

I don't want to go to school (bullying)

Who may hit or pinch or slap or kick as well as name call.

Who threatens people to make them upset.

Optional *Take further ideas and add them if appropriate.*

Look at this list. Have your own thoughts about it. But let it remind you that we know very well what bullying is. We know what people feel like when they are bullied.

How do people who are bullied feel?

● ● ● ● ● ● ● ● ● ● ● ● ●

Let's look at another list.

(Use OHT 2 – uncover each line in turn.)

Here's a person who used to be bullied telling us what they felt like –

When I was bullied at school, this is how it was for me –

I could not get to sleep because I worried about what would happen next day.

I was miserable in the mornings because I was worried about what would happen to me that day.

I would try to go a long way round to school so as not to bump into the people who were bullying me.

I would try to be near the dinner ladies at lunchtime for protection.

I would try to keep away from the bullies in the cloakroom.

I would feel sick in class because I knew the bullies were making faces at me and talking about me.

I would rush out of school to get home in case the bullies were waiting for me.

I would tell lies to my mum and dad about what was happening to me.

I was more unhappy than I have ever been before or since.

Optional *Take further ideas and add them if appropriate.*

You see? We know what it feels like. You aren't alone if you have these feelings. You aren't a peculiar person because you feel like that.

Now, let's leave that list up there for a moment. I want you to look at that list, and I want you to think whether any of the things in that list describe how you feel. I won't ask you to put up your hand. But if you are looking at that list and thinking that it's you, then I want you to make your mind up to tell somebody. Tell your teacher, or another adult in school you trust, or your parents when you get home. Don't keep it to yourself. It's difficult for others to help you if you don't tell someone what's happening to you.

● ● ● ● ● ● ● ● ● ● ●

Now let me tell you a short story. It's about Jerry.

Jerry was bullied almost all the time he was at school. When he was an infant he was locked in the toilet by bigger boys. Even when he was grown up, he still remembered that – the feeling of being locked up and wondering if he would ever get out.

When he was a little older he was called names because he was tall and thin and wore glasses and didn't like football or any other sport. Part of the reason that he didn't like sport was

I don't want to go to school (bullying)

because he wore glasses and he was afraid of getting them broken.

In his secondary school, Jerry was called even more names because older children are often better at thinking of cruel names than younger children are.

But as he grew older still, an interesting thing started to happen. Jerry didn't change. He didn't decide to fight back. Why should he? He wasn't that kind of person. Why should he change when it was the others who were doing the wrong things?

But as he grew older something certainly happened. The people who were bullying him grew older too. And as they grew older, they started to see things that they had not seen before. They saw that even though Jerry was different from them, he was quite an interesting person. He was good at music and he knew a lot of jokes. So instead of bullying him they started listening to him and they grew to like him and to include him in all of the things they did.

Jerry's one and only friend, Carl, had always known that Jerry was kind and interesting, but the others hadn't realised what he was like. They weren't as sensible as Carl and not so quick to see the good in people. What a shame for them, though, that they had missed out on all the good things that Jerry had to offer for all those years.

• • • • • • • • • • •

What can we learn from this story? *Take some suggestions if appropriate.*

There are different ways of bullying people and being bullied is something that you never forget.

Let's think first about how Jerry was being bullied at school. Yes, at first he was locked in the toilets, but he was also being called cruel names. Is that serious do you think? I think it is. Make no mistake, name calling is cruel. Name calling that upsets people is bullying. Why is that? Because your name is important to you. What people call you is important. It can make you feel good, or it can make you feel bad. If someone calls you a name on purpose that makes you feel bad, then that's bullying.

The second thing to think about is why Jerry was being bullied? The story says because he looked a bit different. He didn't like sport either, and that might have been part of it. Let me ask you – does it matter how someone looks? Of course it doesn't. Does it matter if someone doesn't like sport? Of course not. In fact it's good to have people around with different interests. Life would be very boring if we all liked the same things and looked the same, too!

Now, how did Jerry cope with the bullying? The story doesn't really tell us does it? We know that he didn't fight, because he wasn't that kind of a person. He probably just came to accept it as something he had to put up with. He shouldn't have had to do that, should he? Everyone has the right to be themselves. Nobody should be trying to change you into someone else.

Let's think about when the bullying stopped. It was when other people in school started to realise that Jerry was a nice person – someone it was good to talk to and to know.

I want you to think about the advice that you would give to Jerry. I don't know if he told anybody, but I think if he didn't then he should have done. The most important thing

I don't want to go to school (bullying)

if you're being bullied is to tell somebody. Tell your teacher, or another adult in school you trust or your parents. Get it off your chest and you'll feel better straightaway. Then we can stop it happening together.

Use the second half of OHT 1. Uncover one line at at time.

We know what it feels like to be bullied.

We want to help.

You are not alone.

Tell one of us.

We can make it stop.

It's our job to make it stop.

 ## A prayer

Dear God we thank you for the protection of people we love and trust. Help people who bully others to see that they are causing unhappiness and fear. And help anyone in our school who is being bullied to have the courage to tell someone about it. Amen.

A thought

We know that bullying happens. We know that many people can be bullies, perhaps only for a short time. When they think about what they are doing they usually stop. If we remind them of their unkindness then perhaps they will stop doing it.

I don't want to go to school (bullying)

A bully is a person –

Who teases or name calls someone to make them upset.

Who deliberately picks on people who will be upset.

Who may hit or pinch or slap or kick as well as name

call.

Who threatens people to make them upset.

We know what it feels like to be bullied.

We want to help.

You are not alone.

Tell one of us.

We can make it stop.

It's our job to make it stop.

I don't want to go to school (bullying)

When I was bullied at school, this is how it was for me –

I could not get to sleep because I worried about what would happen next day.

I was miserable in the mornings because I was worried about what would happen to me that day.

I would try to go a long way round to school so as not to bump into the people who were bullying me.

I would try to be near the dinner ladies at lunchtime for protection.

I would try to keep away from the bullies in the cloakroom.

I would feel sick in class because I knew the bullies were making faces at me and talking about me.

I would rush out of school to get home in case the bullies were waiting for me.

I would tell lies to my mum and dad about what was happening to me.

I was more unhappy than I have ever been before or since.

Am I a bully?

✦ Introduction

This assembly on bullying focuses on the child who bullies. It's best used after the other bullying assembly which focuses on the victim. Because of that, some phrases and sentences refer back to the first bullying assembly. It's quite possible to use 'Am I a bully?' on its own of course, in which case, you'd need to take care to reword passages that refer back.

Again, the assembly is to use either when there's been concern about particular incidents of bullying or to reinforce the school's bullying policy and approach to bullying and behaviour.

Aims:

The aims of this assembly are to

- demonstrate that the school takes bullying seriously

- bring home to children who are bullying others the seriousness of their actions

- help those children to change their behaviour.

✦ Background

If there has been a bullying incident, or a series of incidents, they will have been dealt with individually as part of the school's behaviour policy. There comes a point, though, where the school's attitude has to be stated publicly in assembly. The idea of this assembly is to help you to do just that – both to reassure children who may be afraid and to let the whole community know that such behaviour will not be tolerated.

An important theme in all bullying policies is to bring home to the bullying child the consequences of his or her behaviour. This is necessary because children who do things that seem to be outrageous often haven't really absorbed their true meaning in the way that an adult might do. So, although the question of punishment is a matter for the school, it's necessary also to talk through consequences – to get bullying children to understand some of the pain that victims feel.

In this context, many teachers are a little uncomfortable with the label 'bully' – though we use it in the assembly both as shorthand and for dramatic effect.

This is because there's something final about it – the idea that a child can be saddled with a word like that. In fact, it's more true to say that a child usually isn't either a bully or not a bully. There are children who bully some of the time – and for some of the time the same children may be 'victims' (another problematic label). It's probably better to talk about 'bullying behaviour'.

It's also true that bullying tends to be done by groups rather than by lone individuals. The group will have leaders and followers. Some of the followers are, essentially, victims, because they are under the influence of the leaders. While bullying policies, assemblies, methods of punishment or counselling and so on can be relatively ineffective against really hard core bullying behaviour, they can certainly separate out some of the followers who already have doubts about what they are doing. This is important in building up a critical mass of children prepared to reject bullying behaviour. And if the leaders become few and isolated then it becomes easier to keep an eye on them and deal with them. This assembly is just one of many strategies that a school can use to remind children who bully of exactly what it is they are doing.

✦ Before the assembly

You will need

- the OHT masters supplied on pages 82, 88–89

- an OHP

- an A4 sheet of paper to mask some of the text.

Inform staff that you are going to give an assembly on bullying.

📖 The assembly

Do we all know what bullying is? *(Refer to the other bullying assembly if that's been used recently.)* Let's remind ourselves.

Display OHT1 from the Bullying 1 assembly.

A bully is a person –

Who teases or name calls someone to make them upset.

Who deliberately picks on people who will be upset.

Who may hit or pinch or slap or kick as well as name call.

Who threatens people to make them upset.

Now let me tell you four very short stories.

Linda and her friends were walking along to school together when they spotted Jack across the road. They started to shout things at him. 'It's little Jack! Hello, little Jack! Why isn't your mummy looking after you, little Jack!' Jack hated being called 'little Jack' and they knew that, so they did it every day, and all the more because he hated it.

Asha was feeling upset because her pet hamster had died. Simone said to her, 'You're a baby, you. Fancy crying about a hamster. You're just a big baby!' Simone kept on and on calling her a baby after that, and persuaded other children in the class to do the same, and Asha got more and more upset.

Jaswinder had bruises all over her ankles. Her mum asked her what they were and she said she had bumped herself in the gym. But really it was because Maxine kicked her hard on the ankles whenever she got near her. She kicked her when she went past in class, and she kicked her if she was standing next to her in the line for dinner. Jaswinder tried to keep out of Maxine's way, but she couldn't keep out of the way all the time.

Morgan went up to Will and said 'Will, I'm going to get you after school.' All that day Will was frightened, and when it came time to go home, he rushed to get out of school before Morgan and he forgot his coat. He ran all the way home, looking behind him to see if

Am I a bully?

Morgan was coming. He got home earlier than usual and his mum asked him why, and told him off for forgetting his coat. But Will didn't tell his mum the real reason. And then the same thing happened next day, and the next.

- - - - - - - - - - - -

Now imagine you could speak to Linda, and Simone, and Maxine and Morgan. Imagine you said to each of them 'You are a bully.'

Linda would probably say 'I'm not a bully. I was just calling Jack names. Everybody does it. It doesn't mean anything.'

Simone would probably say 'I'm not a bully. I just can't stand people who cry all the time. Nobody likes people who cry all the time.'

Maxine would probably say 'I'm not a bully. I don't really hit Jaswinder. I just give her a little kick because she annoys me.'

Morgan would probably say 'I'm not a bully. I was just teasing Will. Everybody does it. It doesn't mean anything.'

You see? People who bully don't think they are bullying. 'I'm not a bully!' they say. 'I'm just having a laugh!' or 'I just do it because she annoys me!'

What they haven't done, though, is think about how it feels to be on the receiving end. That's what a bully is really – someone who doesn't understand or care about another person's feelings.

So are you a bully? Ask yourself these questions.

- - - - - - - - - - - -

Display OHT 1 for this assembly.

Have you ever threatened to get someone after school, and kept on threatening them even though you knew it frightened them?

Have you ever joined in calling someone cruel names?

Have you ever hidden someone's coat, or bag, or other things on purpose, and kept on doing it when you saw that it made them angry and upset?

Have you ever persuaded someone not to be friends with somebody else?

Are you doing any of these things?

Are you in a group that's doing these things?

Are you friends with someone who does these things?

If the answer is yes, then at the moment you are a bully. You may say that you're not, but your behaviour says that you are.

Now, you may not always be a bully. You may not have been a bully yesterday. You may not be a bully tomorrow. But right now you are a bully, I'm afraid. So if that's you, let me ask you to think about what it feels like to be bullied.

- - - - - - - - - - - -

Display OHT 2.

Being bullied means –

Being afraid on the playground or in the cloakroom.

Going home the long way round.

Being late for school to avoid being bullied.

© **pfp** 2002 ISBN 1 874050 57 0 May be photocopied for use only within the purchasing institution **pfp**, 61 Gray's Inn Road, London WC1X 8TH

Am I a bully?

Thinking about being bullied and not being able to get to sleep.

Not being able to tell your parents what's the matter.

Telling lies to your parents about what's happening.

Being more unhappy than you have ever been.

• • • • • • • • • • • •

Would you like to feel like that?

Do you really want to make other people feel like that?

Because that's what you are doing if you bully people.

If you keep on being nasty to one person because you know it frightens them or annoys them, then that's bullying. You don't have to be hitting them – you know as well as I do that you can be upset and frightened by words even if nobody hurts you.

If you go around with someone who does a lot of bullying, and if you join in, or even if you do nothing to stop it, then that's bullying too.

• • • • • • • • • • • •

If you're doing any of these things, then it's time to stop. It's time to show some courage and refuse to join in bullying. You know the difference between right and wrong. You know it's not right to keep on upsetting someone just because it seems to be fun, or because someone else tells you to do it. So make sure you do something today to put things right. Don't put it off or wait till somebody gets so upset that it makes them ill. Do something about it today.

☀ A prayer

Lord, you teach us to love our neighbours. That's a hard thing to ask us, and we don't always manage it. But we shouldn't do the opposite, and behave as if we hate people, or as if we like to upset people. We know that's wrong, and we ask you to help us not to do it, no matter how we are tempted or persuaded. Give us strength and self-respect. Amen.

☀ A thought

People who bully find it difficult to do it without an audience. If all the followers of the bully walked away when bullying behaviour started and didn't support the bully, then bullying would stop, and life would be easier for everyone.

Am I a bully?

Have you ever threatened to get someone after school, and kept on threatening them even though you knew it frightened them?

Have you ever joined in calling someone cruel names?

Have you ever hidden someone's coat, or bag, or other things on purpose, and kept on doing it when you saw that it made them angry and upset?

Have you ever persuaded someone not to be friends with somebody else?

Are you doing any of these things?

Are you in a group that's doing these things?

Are you friends with someone who does these things?

Being bullied means –

Being afraid on the playground or in the cloakroom.

Going home the long way round.

Being late for school to avoid being bullied.

Thinking about being bullied and not being able to get to sleep.

Not being able to tell your parents what's the matter.

Telling lies to your parents about what's happening.

Being more unhappy than you have ever been.

Am I a bully? • OHT 2

Cruelty to animals

✦ Introduction

Just occasionally, you may have to deal with an incident in which some pupils have been cruel to an animal. This assembly helps raise the issue in general terms and provides a specific follow-up with the individual children involved. It requires some brief preparation – see 'Before the assembly' below.

Aims:

The aims of this assembly are to

- present the facts to the whole school

- reassure children who are upset, that this bad behaviour is totally unacceptable and will be dealt with

- help the specific children to realise they have behaved badly and to consider the consequences

- help all children understand their responsibilities to living creatures and the environment.

✦ Background

Often a complaint about cruelty to animals will come from other pupils, who may, for example, have seen boys and girls throwing frogs about or throwing stones at swimming birds. These children will almost certainly be upset by the incident and need reassurance that you are going to do something about it.

This uncaring behaviour does need to be dealt with. However, it does not call for a highly charged and outraged response. Children who do this kind of thing are not usually being deliberately sadistic. Their behaviour is typical of the kind of thoughtlessness of growing children – they have not considered their actions, nor had the consequences properly pointed out to them. This assembly, therefore, is to help them to think, and to see what it is that they are doing. In addition, it is a good idea to use this time to help all pupils to understand what responsibilities we all have towards the rest of the living world.

Any child who then carries on being deliberately and persistently cruel has a particular need that has to be dealt with individually – it can sometimes indicate more deep-rooted problems and may be part of a general behaviour pattern.

✦ Before the assembly

You will need

- the supplied OHT master (page 94)

- an overhead projector

- two A4 sheets of paper to mask some of the illustrations as indicated.

Cruelty to animals

📖 The assembly

I'm going to show you some pictures today, and I'm going to ask you some questions about each of them.

Cover all the pictures except the one named.

After each question leave time for responses from the pupils before stating the final answer. Some questions require only simple yes or no responses, but some ask for more specific answers from the pupils.

• • • • • • • • • • •

Uncover the picture of the child.

What is this a picture of? A child.

Can this child tell me things? Yes.

If she is hurt, can she feel the pain? Yes.

Can she tell me when she is feeling ill, or has a pain? Yes.

Could another person hurt her if he or she wanted to? Yes.

Should another person hurt her? No.

Why not? *(Take some individual answers.)* Because she has done no harm, and in any case hurting her is not a sensible way of dealing with anything that she has done. Our duty is to look after her, isn't it?

What do we think of the behaviour of people who deliberately hurt children? We don't like that sort of behaviour at all.

• • • • • • • • • • •

Uncover the picture of the baby.

Let me ask you the same questions.

Can this baby tell me things? *(Take some individual answers.)* Well … in a way. She can cry and I might work out why she is crying. She can smile and make happy noises. But she can't speak to me yet, and tell me things.

If she is hurt can she feel it? Yes.

Can she tell me when she is feeling ill or has a pain? Only by crying, not by speaking.

Could another person hurt her if he or she wanted to? Very easily. The baby is very delicate and easily hurt.

Should another person hurt her? Definitely not. Our duty is to look after her.

What do we think of the behaviour of people who deliberately hurt babies? We don't like that sort of behaviour at all.

• • • • • • • • • • •

Uncover the picture of the dog.

Now let me ask you the same questions about this dog.

Can this dog tell me things? Well, in a very limited way he can make signals about wanting some food. He can jump up and down when I get his lead to go for a walk – he's telling me he's pleased and excited then.

Can you think of any other ways he can tell me things? *(Take some individual answers.)*

If he is hurt can he feel it? Yes.

Can he tell me when he is ill or in pain? Yes, by his behaviour and sounds.

Could a person hurt this dog? Very easily. He's a small dog and easily hurt.

Cruelty to animals

Should a person hurt this dog? No. The dog is a living creature who is part of our natural world, and we have a duty to look after him.

What do we think of the behaviour of people who hurt dogs? We don't like that sort of behaviour at all.

Uncover the picture of the rabbit.

Now, how about this wild rabbit? Can she tell me things? In a very limited way she can make signals about hunger or pain. But that's all.

If she is hurt can she feel it? Yes.

Can she tell me when she is ill, or in pain? Perhaps, in a limited way, by her behaviour and sounds.

Could a person hurt this rabbit? Very easily. She's a small rabbit and easily hurt.

Should a person hurt this rabbit? *(Take some individual answers.)* No. This is a wild rabbit. We have no business hurting her – although some people might want to kill her for food. Even then, they would not want to hurt her for no reason.

What do we think of the behaviour of people who unnecessarily hurt rabbits? We don't like that sort of behaviour at all.

Uncover the picture of the frog.

And what about this frog? Can he tell me things? Probably not. I don't know much about how frogs communicate.

But if he is hurt can he feel it? Yes.

Can he tell me when he is ill or in pain? Perhaps only by trying to get away.

Could a person hurt this frog? *(Take some individual answers.)* Very easily. He's small and easily hurt.

Should a person hurt this frog? No. The frog is part of nature and is important in the balance of our world, and in any case we have no business hurting a small wild creature like this frog.

What do we think of the behaviour of people who hurt frogs? We don't like that sort of behaviour at all.

Uncover the picture of the duck.

Can this duck tell me things? *(Take some individual answers.)* In a very limited way, by her behaviour or sounds, she can make signals to me about hunger or pain. But that's all.

But if she is hurt can she feel it? Yes, of course.

Could a person hurt this duck? Very easily. She's a small duck and easily hurt.

Should a person hurt this duck? No. The duck is another living creature in our world, and we have the duty to look after her.

What do we think of the behaviour of people who hurt ducks? We don't like that sort of behaviour at all.

Cruelty to animals

Pause. Make sure all the pictures on the OHT are now visible.

Now – nobody would want to hurt another child or a baby would they? Is it different to hurt an animal? A dog? A rabbit? A duck? A frog?

In some ways it is different. A rabbit is not a human being. A frog is not a human being. A person who hurts a child or a baby is in more serious trouble than a person who hurts a frog or a duck.

But the person who hurts a frog or a duck is still in trouble – it's still something the police take action about. Why is that?

Because like a baby or another child, a duck or a frog or a rabbit is a living creature that shares the Earth with us, and we have the duty of not hurting other living creatures unnecessarily. After all, we are supposed to be the clever ones.

Are you cleverer than a rabbit? Or a duck? Or a frog? Of course you are. That means you're supposed to be sensible enough not to do anything to hurt a creature which shares the Earth with us and which does us no harm.

Of course, human beings do kill animals. They kill them for food, and occasionally they kill them for sport. You must make up your minds about this. Many people will not eat animal meat because they do not believe in killing for food. Others protest against hunting. Make up your own mind.

But let me remind you that even those who kill for food or for sport are very much against straight cruelty to animals – the causing of unnecessary suffering.

So, if you see people throwing stones at the ducks, or playing games with defenceless and harmless creatures, then just think it through – is this something you want to do? Will it make you seem more clever or more responsible? Or will it make you look a little silly and irresponsible?

☀ **A prayer**

Dear God, who made this beautiful world, help us to remember that all living things are part of your creation and that we should care for animals and not hurt them or be cruel to them. Amen.

☀ **A thought**

We are all part of a world where animals and plants live alongside us and give us great pleasure in their beauty. Let's remember that they should be cared for, and not harmed, and that we have a duty to look after them and not hurt them.

Cruelty to animals

Cruelty to animals • OHT pfp

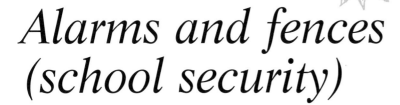

Alarms and fences (school security)

✦ Introduction

This assembly is to help allay worries about school security, particularly when security work is going on or about to happen in a school.

Aims:

The aims of this assembly are to

- reassure pupils that they can feel safe in school

- let pupils know that the security work is to make them feel even safer

- reassure pupils that the fact that extra security is being added to the school does not mean that they are in any danger there.

✦ Background

Children and their parents wonder about their safety in school. Publicity about intruders, and vandalism or arson attacks, and the discussion that follows such incidents, raise anxieties in the minds of pupils which they may not openly express.

These worries can actually be heightened when things start happening at school to improve security – the installation of cameras, for example, or the erection of boundary fencing and security gates – as it can give the impression that it is an unsafe place to be. If this kind of work is about to happen, or is going on in your school, this assembly will help you to allay any fears that children and parents may be harbouring.

✦ Before the assembly

Optional Make a list of any security works being undertaken on an OHT.

📖 The assembly

Is your house a safe and cosy place? I hope so. I hope it's a good place where all your family can go and feel secure. A place where you can go in and close the door. You can close the curtains if you want, too. You can even lock the door – and the windows – and nobody can come in unless you want them to. You can feel safe and snug in your home with your family.

Is school like that? I hope so. It's our job to make it like that – a place where you can come and know that all your friends are here and all your teachers, and you can feel safe and comfortable.

Just recently, we've decided to make our school even safer than it is already. We've had to think a lot about that, because we can't keep school locked up so much that no visitors or parents can get in and out. We want people to feel welcome, but we do want to make sure that school is a safe place.

That's why we've decided to do some work to make it even more snug and safe than it is now.

Optional *Display your OHT and explain what work is taking place.*

Alarms and fences (school security)

I don't think anyone would come in to harm you, but they might come in to steal things, or to take the teachers' handbags or car keys. So, just like we keep people out of our houses who shouldn't be in there, we're doing the same at school.

We're making sure that we're safe in here all together.

Let me tell you some little stories about being safe in school.

First let me tell you about Jamie.

One day Jamie's teacher asked him to go to the office to take a note to the secretary. So off he went down the corridor and through the entrance hall to the office. He delivered the note, and the secretary said, 'Thank you, Jamie,' and he set off back to his classroom.

As he was passing through the entrance hall he saw a lady waiting at the door of the school to come in. Now Jamie was a polite boy so he decided to let the lady in. So he reached up for the catch on the door. It was a bit high and he couldn't reach it, so he looked around and there in the enrance hall was a chair. He went and got the chair and put it by the door and climbed up on it so he could reach the latch. 'I'll be able to let the lady in now,' he said to himself. 'I want to be helpful because she is a visitor to our school.'

But before he could turn the latch on the door, the secretary came out and said, 'Jamie! What are you doing? You know you shouldn't do that.'

Now can anyone tell me why Jamie shouldn't have been doing that?

(Answers may be – he shouldn't be standing on a chair, he shouldn't be letting someone in who is waiting for an adult to answer the door or release the automatic catch.)

The reason he had to stand on a chair was because the door latch was too high. And why was it too high? Because the headteacher didn't want children letting people in that nobody knew.

So, you see, Jamie was being polite and trying to be helpful, but he shouldn't let people into school that he doesn't know.

Luckily, the secretary found another way for Jamie to be helpful. The secretary let the lady in, because she knew who she was, and so she asked Jamie to go and get the headteacher for her. 'Jamie, I think Mrs Tasker is in the Hall talking to the dinner ladies. Will you go and tell her that her visitor has arrived?'

Jamie was pleased that he'd been asked to do something helpful and off he went to find Mrs Tasker.

Here's another story about being safe in school.

In the next town, the police were very concerned because two men were going around stealing. And what they were doing was going into places where people worked and looking for handbags or briefcases that had been left lying about. Sometimes men or women leave the place where they are working for a few minutes – maybe to go to the toilet or to get a drink – and these men were

Alarms and fences (school security)

watching for handbags that had been left behind, and they were stealing them.

How could they do it? Because they dressed so that nobody suspected them. If they were going into an office, they put suits on and carried their own briefcases, and everyone thought they were visiting businessmen. If it was a factory where people wore overalls, then they put overalls on, and everybody thought they were from a different part of the factory. Nobody went up to them and said, 'Excuse me who are you and what are you doing here?' That's what they should have done.

Well, the police were worried that these men would come into schools to do the same thing. The police chief inspector rang up the headteachers and said, 'They might come in during assembly when everyone is in the hall, or they might come in when there's a meeting in the staffroom after school. Then they'll walk round looking for handbags and briefcases.'

So the headteachers were ready – they were able to warn their teachers not to leave their bags lying about, and they always had somebody in the office, watching the door. So the thieves never came into school. But it made the headteachers realise that they ought to put in some of the safety precautions that we are putting into our school now. It's better to be safe than sorry.

Pause.

☀ A prayer

Dear God, we thank you for the safety of our homes and the other secure places we all know and like being in. Thank you, too, for our school which is also a safe place in which we feel we belong. We pray that the new work going on will make us even safer. We know that it will protect us and make school a place where we can relax and feel comfortable. Amen.

☀ A thought

We belong here. All of us – all of you, all the teachers, all the other people who work here, and your parents when they come to see us. We all belong here. We want to feel safe here. We don't want anyone coming in who doesn't belong. So we're making ourselves even more safe than we were before. We can come into school and relax and feel comfortable, because we know we will be alright here. We know that it will protect us.

Confirmation of the school's closure

✦ Introduction

The closure of a school always has considerable sadness attached to it. This assembly is intended for use at a suitable point in the lead up to a closure and not as a valedictory assembly to use when a school actually closes. It requires some brief preparation – see 'Before the assembly' below.

Aims:

The aims of this assembly are to

- present pupils with whatever facts are known about the future of their school

- reassure them that the things they fear the worst – such as the immediate closure of their school, for example – are not going to happen

- let pupils know that you will not allow their interests to be forgotten

- encourage pupils to believe that new starts can be made.

✦ Background

A school closure does not happen suddenly – arguments about the school's future can be long and drawn out, often to the detriment of morale and pupil progress.

However, there will invariably be key stages as the situation develops – the morning that the issue first arises, for example, or the day that the decision to close down is made definite. On such days there will be worry and unrest among the children, often fed by similar feelings among parents and staff. This is when children need to be reassured, and to be helped to realise that nothing is going to happen to them immediately, and that they will not be forgotten in the midst of any dispute that may develop.

While some children will accept the news easily, and experience only minimal distress, others will probably experience a number of adjustment problems. The children's responses may range from depression to anger. These children will need to work through these feelings such as in small group discussions or through the use of art as therapy and so on.

✦ Before the assembly

Make a note of all the facts you know are public knowledge. Write them down so that you have a record of exactly what everyone has been told, and so that you know you haven't missed anything. You can also then use this list for a letter to parents, so that you can be sure everyone is getting the same information.

Hold a brief staff meeting beforehand, to make sure that the staff know everything you are about to say – it may be a shock if some of them have missed key information and only find it out as you tell the children.

Confirmation of the school's closure

📖 **The assembly**

I want to talk to you today about something I'm sure is important to you all – it's also very important to me – the future of our school, and that it is going to close.

Let me tell you straightaway what I know.

Say the facts carefully and clearly.

Now, let me tell you what is not going to happen.

First, the school is not going to close tomorrow *(or next week, or next month, whatever you know for sure)*. Things like this take a long time to organise. Many of you will have moved on to other schools before it happens. So even though you will hear a lot of talk about the closing of the school, and even though your parents and teachers will be discussing it, I don't want you to think that something dreadful is going to happen very suddenly, because it's not like that at all.

I also want to tell you that in all our plans we are not going to forget you and your education. All of that will be very much on our minds. Our school is all about you – your happiness and welfare, and your progress in the classroom. I promise you that none of us will forget that.

Here's a story to remind us of that. It's not about a school closing. But it's about somebody who had to make a much bigger new start.

• • • • • • • • • • • •

Jan was a schoolgirl, about your age, when she suddenly faced a big change in her life. Her school didn't close, but the change was just as big for her. What happened was that her family had to leave the town where they had always lived. In fact, not only did they have to leave their town, they had to leave their country.

Sometimes these things happen and a family find that they can no longer earn a living, or be free to do what they want in the country where they have always lived. Certainly that's what happened to Jan's parents. The government changed, and the new government started to put into prison those people who belonged to the political parties who disagreed with them.

So one night, Jan's dad came home and said, 'We're going right now. It's too dangerous to stay here.'

So they loaded up their car. And as they were loading it up, who should come to the house but Jan's teacher.

Jan liked her teacher very much, and knew that she would miss her. She liked the little school, with its old, worn wooden desks and the stove in the corner of the room. She liked her friends, and her books, and the stories that they all shared. And when she saw her teacher that night, she cried.

'Don't cry, Jan,' said her teacher. 'Take this with you, and you'll always have something of us to remember us by.' She gave Jan a cardboard box tied with string.

The car was loaded up, and the family headed for the border. They crossed two other countries over the next three days and then came to a port. There they boarded a ship, and made a five-day journey to a new country where they could find freedom – America.

Jan was completely bewildered. She missed her friends and her old home.

Confirmation of the school's closure

But the time quickly came when Jan had to go to a new school – a school in a new town, in a new country. She was tearful on the first morning, and her mum comforted her. Then her mum had a thought. 'What happened to the box?' she said to Jan.

Jan knew immediately what she meant. 'The box from my teacher! I forgot all about it!'

She found it among all the belongings that were piled up in the spare room. Together, they opened it. Inside were all of Jan's books from her old school – her writing book and her maths book, and some of her drawings, and a bible and a book of stories. And on top there was a letter from her teacher.

'Dear Jan,' it said. 'You have learned many things with me, but the most important thing is that you have learned to look outwards – to see that there is a big world, full of good people, that there are new books to read, new things to learn, new people to meet. Go out and meet them, Jan. Be brave and don't let us down. Take these books with you, and keep them with you always, because they will remind you of how we were together, and that we will always think of you.'

So Jan dried her eyes, and picked up her box and headed off for her new school. And that morning her new American teacher stood Jan before the class and said,

'Class, this is Jan. Like so many people in our country she has come with her parents from far away, and she feels uncertain and afraid. But she's just shown me her books and I know she has been well taught by a good teacher. I am proud to carry on where her teacher left off, and I know you will make her welcome.'

So Jan made a new start, and grew up to be a proud citizen of a new country. But she kept her old school books with her to the end of her days, and many times as she grew old she would go to her sideboard and get out her old teacher's letter and carefully unfold it and read it again.

'New people to meet,' she said to herself. 'I certainly met lots of new people. And it turned out very well in the end.'

'What was that, dear?' said her husband from his chair across the room. 'Are you reading that old letter again?'

Jan smiled at him, and he went back to his newspaper.

Pause.

New starts are difficult, and the feelings we have are mixed – there is sadness, some fear, some excitement. But if we have taught you well, then you will be ready for whatever comes – and a new school can be a new opportunity.

Finally, let me tell you that I will keep you up-to-date with what is happening. I will tell you things in assembly, and I will send letters home to your parents. If you have any questions, don't hesitate to ask me. If you have fears and worries, then come and share them with me or your teachers. And pass that message on to your parents and families too – if they have worries and questions, then come and ask at school about them.

Now let's have a quiet moment together.

Pause, and then continue.

Confirmation of the school's closure

☀ A prayer

Dear God, help us not to worry too much about the future. Let us remember that we are here together and that we can help and support each other. Help us to share our concerns and face any problems together. We know that we will always have the love of our friends and our families. Help us to really enjoy the time that we have together now, and to look forward with excitement to what may happen in the future. Amen.

☀ A thought

We are worried today – a bit uncertain about the future, wondering if things are going to change for us. But for a while, let's let the future take care of itself, and let's remind ourselves of a few things that might be of help to us. We are here together and we can support each other. Other people share our concerns, and we can face them together. Nothing is going to happen suddenly. We will have time to prepare ourselves for whatever happens. And all the time we will have the love of our friends and families. Those things will always be there. We will enjoy the time that we can spend together now and then we will be able to look forward to the future with hope and excitement.

Divorce and separation

✦ Introduction

Many children are affected by divorce and separation. Occasionally, a school may find it appropriate to address this issue either as part of the normal PSHE programme, or as a response to a situation where some children have been making unkind comments to or bullying a child whose parents have separated or recently divorced.

Aims:

The aims of this assembly are to

- reassure the children that parental separation happens to other families as well as their own

- remind the children that parents who no longer want to be together will still continue to love their children

- reassure the children that they are not to blame when separation happens.

✦ Background

Around one in eight children in primary schools is likely to experience divorce and there's doubt over whether it has a big impact on them. Younger children, in particular, often simply don't understand what is happening to their parents, which makes them feel confused, angry and afraid.

Children also often feel guilt – their lack of understanding often leads children to think that the break up is somehow their fault – and helplessness, which in turn easily leads to a feeling of worthlessness. This can manifest itself in different ways depending on the child, but most of these ways will cause their school work to be affected.

The task for the school then is to provide both care, affection and understanding, and clear and steady expectations about work and behaviour.

It is important, therefore, to deal with these children as honestly as possible, providing accurate information and reassurance to try to head off any feelings of guilt and fear.

There is important work that teachers need to do with children individually at such times, but this assembly will help you to put all that work in a wider context. It will help you let all the children know that neither divorce nor the feelings that are generated by it are unusual, that you and the staff understand and that the school as a community can provide support and stability in such times of change.

If possible, try not to do the assembly at a time when a child is right in the middle of a separation or divorce – if this is the case, it will be best to wait a while before raising the issue with a large group.

(There are extended notes on how teachers can help children through divorce in Appendix 1, page 145, and a list of further resources and organisations in Appendix 3, Divorce on page 148.)

Divorce and separation

✦ Before the assembly

Check with the staff to try to ensure that no child has very recently experienced their parents' divorce or separation.

📖 The assembly

Do you know, one of the really interesting things about people is that they like being together. You only have to look around a school to know that. Even when we have free time to go where we want, at break for example, we usually choose to gather together in groups. Sometimes a person wants to be alone, but most of the time we are in groups, or pairs, just talking and joking and playing – enjoying being together.

We like the comfort of being with other people, in assembly, in the playground, and in the staffroom.

When you look more closely at these groups in school, though, you will find that they change as time goes on. Some people drift away to be members of other groups. Friendships come and go. In the staffroom the groups change, too – a teacher wants to go and work somewhere else, or retires, and a new teacher comes along.

Now think about people being married. That means really liking to be together! A man and a woman get married, perhaps when they are quite young, and often they stay together for many years (probably until one of them dies).

That's usually a very long time, and it's not easy to stay together like that. When you think about it, in all that time these two people are bound to have disagreements along the way. Some will be serious, others will be trivial, and some trivial ones will get blown up so that they seem to be serious.

Often people talk about marriage as if it were a road. People travel along it and there are both easy times and difficulties on the way, just as there might be as you go on a long journey. There is bad weather, rocky bits sometimes, traffic jams. Often these cause a few hiccups or delays, but people usually get to the other end.

But sometimes, though, when people make a journey, the going gets a bit too difficult. They try hard. They keep trying to work out the best route. But in the end they decide that the best thing is simply not to carry on.

Some marriages turn out like that. The going gets difficult. The disagreements between a husband and wife become serious. The couple try hard to sort things out. But in the end they decide that they are spending more time on their problems than they are on anything else.

When that happens they sometimes think that perhaps the best thing to do is not to go on. So they decide to live apart. It's very sad when that happens – after all when they got married they were very happy and were ready to stay together for the rest of their lives. But the couple may feel that parting is better than trying to stay together, when each of them has changed so that they don't have much fun together any more.

Divorce and separation

Now there's one important factor in all of this that I haven't mentioned.

When the married couple started off on their journey, usually there was just the two of them – a couple. But as the journey went on, usually others came along – children. They had children because they wanted them, and when the children came they both loved them very much.

And when the bad moments and the disagreements started, they usually tried hard not to let it affect the children, because whatever they thought about each other, they continued to love their children. Dad was still Dad. Mum was still Mum. Even if they eventually decided to part, they still each love their children just as much as ever.

Children sometimes find it difficult to sort all of this out in their minds. They sometimes think that if their parents have stopped loving each other, then maybe they don't feel the same about their children. But when you think about it, a dad who loves his children, or a mum who loves her children, is still going to go on loving them, whatever happens. It's not the children who have made things difficult. In fact, the children may have often made things a little easier. If adults can't get on very well together, then the fact that there are children can sometimes help them – it's always helpful to have someone else to love and to talk to.

. . . .

So when parents part, they still love their children. Sometimes it's more difficult to show it, because one parent is not in the house all the time. But the love is still there.

Children sometimes feel that they might have caused the trouble. In fact that's not the case at all. Children are not to blame when parents split up.

Family arguments and separations are very upsetting. There's no getting round that. But they do, happen from time to time. When they do I want you all to remember to be kind and helpful to any children you know who are part of it – imagine how you'd feel if your mum and dad parted. Any child who is affected can tell you that it's very upsetting. It's the same for all children in separated families – and there are quite a few. What children have to do when this happens is remember four things.

Here they are.

When Mum and Dad split up –

- It's upsetting for everybody. No good pretending that it isn't. There will probably be tears. There might even be anger.

- When Mum and Dad stop feeling the same towards each other, they definitely do not stop loving their children. Mum is still Mum. Dad is still Dad. In fact the love between parents and children can grow even stronger.

- After a period of time apart, Mum and Dad can often be happier.

- It's not the children's fault. Nothing they did made the separation happen.

. . . .

Divorce and separation

Here's a short story about a little girl whose Mum and Dad were separating.

Janette was unhappy. She felt as though she had been unhappy for a long time. And she was doing what she usually did when she felt unhappy, which was talk to her grandad down at his flat.

'I feel really miserable, Grandad,' said Janette.

Her grandad sat down and gave her a hug. 'Now, before you go any further, Jan. Let me say two things. First, I feel a bit down, too. And second, that I'm really glad you're telling me about how miserable you are and not bottling it up inside.'

Janette smiled. Grandad had a knack of saying the right thing.

He gave her another hug. 'I know you're miserable about your mum and dad splitting up.'

Janette nodded and her eyes filled with tears. 'Why can't they stay together like you and Gran. You've been together for much longer.'

'Well, Jan,' said Grandad. 'It doesn't always work like that. Your mum and dad have talked and talked and they've tried to keep things together. But it was getting to the point where it was damaging everybody's lives. So we just have to accept that they're doing what they think is right for them.'

Janette bit her lip. 'Is it me, do you think? Am I in the way or something?'

Her grandad looked at her. 'Bless you, Jan. That's not the way it is at all. Your mum and dad love you more than you will ever know. Your dad is going to miss seeing you every day. I know he'll still see quite a lot of you, but the worst thing about this change for him is that he won't be coming home to you each evening, or tucking you up in bed. It's really causing him a lot of sadness. And your mum feels sad for him, too. It's a good job you're there, because you will love them both, at times when they need a lot of love.'

'But what can I do?' asked Janette.

'Now, you must realise, Jan, that you don't have to do anything at all other than what you're already doing. What's happened is not your fault, and you don't have to try to put anything right. Just remember that your mum and dad still love you and you love them. It's not going to be easy in the coming months, but you still have them both, even if it won't be the same.'

Jan dried her eyes. She was still upset. And her grandad was still upset. But Jan was starting to realise that things like this sometimes happen, and that she shouldn't feel guilty. And maybe, after a while, they could all be a bit happier.

☀ A prayer

Dear God, we know that you want families to be happy and to love each other. But we know that not all families manage to stay together. When things go wrong, please be with the people who are upset, and help them to avoid feeling bitter and angry. Amen.

☀ A thought

We all want families to be happy and to love each other. But we know that not all families can manage to stay together. When things go wrong, let's all try and help the people who are upset, and look forward to a time when everyone involved is happier.

Different families

✦ Introduction

Frequently the image of a 'family' portrayed to children is of a married couple with children. For many of our pupils this image does not apply. This assembly uses a visual focus and a short story to explore different sorts of family structures. It requires some brief preparation – see 'Before the assembly' below.

Aims:

The aims of this assembly are to

- show pupils that the word family show a range of possibilities

- show pupils that the essential ingredient is love and care

- show pupils that a changed family can still be a secure family.

✦ Background

In any school there will be a wide range of family structures. For young children the norm will be whatever structure they live in, whether it includes a mum and dad, a single parent, a step-parent, grandparents or, perhaps, a single sex couple and so on. Only as they get older – perhaps by Year 5 – will they begin to contrast and compare themselves with others, and in some cases, maybe start to think that their 'family' is different from the norm.

If the school and home have developed a sense of tolerance and self-esteem in the child this is not usually a problem. But many children are made fun of if their family is somehow different or unusual, such as if one parent is disabled or if they live with same sex parents. This can cause a lot of worry and upset for the children involved.

More often the difficulty comes when family structures break down and relationships within the family are radically affected. In this assembly pupils are given the chance to reflect on a wide range of families and identify with their own situation in a positive way.

(Appendix 1, on page 145, gives further information on the effect of divorce and separation on children.)

✦ Before the assembly

You will need

- the two supplied OHT masters on pages 109–110. The pictures on OHT 2 are to use as overlays to OHT 1 – you will need to cut them out so that they can be used separately. It might need a little practise!

- an overhead projector.

If possible, try to make sure that you are not doing this assembly when a separation has recently occurred in one of the children's families.

📖 The assembly

Show OHT 1 and overlay it with the images on OHT 2 as you tell the story.

Today I'm going to tell you a story about a family. While I'm telling you, I want you to think about this question – 'What is a family?'

Tim and Jess lived in a flat with their mum and dad. There were just the four of them – mum, dad, and two children.

They did all the things that families like that seem to do. Mum and Dad went out to work, though Mum worked part-time so she could get home in time to walk up to the school to meet the children.

It was a busy life for Tim and Jess's mum and dad. Mum seemed to have to hurry all the time – to get the children ready for school, to get to work, to get home, to get to school to meet the children, to get home again and then get everybody's tea ready. Then there was housework and washing and shopping to do. No wonder Mum was tired a lot of the time, and got bad tempered with everybody.

Tim and Jess's dad worked on an industrial estate on the edge of the next town. He had to leave at six-thirty in the morning to be picked up by a special bus, and the bus dropped him back at the end of the road at six o'clock in the evening. So none of the family saw him in the morning, and in the evening he would usually have his evening meal on his own while the others were watching the television, or the children were catching up with their homework.

Tim and Jess knew it was a hard life, but everything seemed to be going well. They enjoyed school, and their mum and dad spent as much time with them as they were able to.

Then, quite suddenly, everything seemed to change. Their dad decided to go and live somewhere else, and their mum was left on her own. So now there was Mum, and Tim and Jess – just the three of them.

That made life even harder. After a while, Tim and Jess's gran came to stay, because she had decided that their mum was finding life on her own too much of a struggle. So their gran stayed in the house all day, and that was quite good, because the tea was ready when they all got home, and the washing was done and so was the housework.

So now in the house there were Tim and Jess and their mum and their gran – four people once again.

All the same, there were some problems, because Tim and Jess found that their gran was quite strict about things like watching the TV and going to bed early. She was stricter than Mum and Dad had been, and they weren't used to it.

Still, everyone settled down together.

Then, after a while, everything changed again. Tim and Jess's mum found a new friend and after a while he moved into the house. He had a little boy of his own called Jack, who was a bit younger than Tim and Jess. And, of course, Gran was still there, too.

So for a time there were six people in the house – Tim and Jess, their mum, their mum's new friend, his son Jack and Gran.

It was OK, but it wasn't a really happy time, because the house was crowded. Everyone was getting used to each other, but they didn't always all get on.

Different families

But, eventually, Gran went back home, and the five remaining people – Tim, Jess, their mum, their mum's new friend, and his son Jack – settled down quite well together.

And then, would you believe it, along came somebody else! Who do you think it was?

Yes, a baby! Tim and Jess's mum had a baby, so they had a new little sister. And there were six people in the house again – Tim and Jess and their mum, and their mum's friend, and his son Jack, and the new baby, Zoe. The house was really crowded again, but everyone was so happy about the new baby that it didn't seem to matter too much. And Mum and her friend were planning on getting a bigger house, so they knew they would soon have a bit more room.

Now, do you remember the question I asked you before I told the story? 'What is a family?'

What do you think? Well, I think it's a group of people living and loving each other in a house. There's usually at least one grown-up, and at least one child. But there may be more, of course.

I think a family needs at least one adult to make it work. An adult cares for the children, probably earns some money, does the household jobs and generally runs the house.

An adult is also the focus for love in the house – the children love their mum, or their dad, or their step-parent, or their grandparent, or all of them, and that adult loves and cares for the children in return. And if there is more than one adult, then the adults will love each other too.

So that's what a family is, I think. I think it's a group of people in a house who love and care for each other.

Optional *Using the OHT images, and with the children's suggestions, make various combinations that could make up a family. Whether or not you show single sex couples with children is a matter for your own school policy, but the possibility is there.*

A prayer

Dear God, help us to appreciate our families and the love that binds them together. We all have different kinds of families, with different kinds and numbers of adults and children in them, but we are thankful for the way that in each of these different kinds of families everyone is able to love and care for each other. Amen.

A thought

Let's think about our own families. Let's think about the love that binds them together – the love between the adults and the children, for example. Adults show their love by the care they give and the hard work they put into running the house. Children show their love by being considerate and knowing how to support the adults when there are difficulties, and also by providing good humour and laughter when it's called for. Whoever the people are that make up our families, let's celebrate the love and care and support that they are able to give each other.

© **pfp** 2002 ISBN 1 874050 57 0 May be photocopied for use only within the purchasing institution **pfp**, 61 Gray's Inn Road, London WC1X 8TH

Different families • page OHT 1

109

Different families

Different families • OHT 2

Parents working away from home

✦ Introduction

This assembly addresses the issue of parents who work away from home for any extended length of time. As an increasing number of trades and professions require worker mobility this is an issue which affects many children. There is an optional section that will require some brief preparation should you choose to use it – see 'Before the assembly' below.

Aims:

The aims of this assembly are to

- let children know that when a parent works away from home it is usually out of necessity and the desire to care properly for the family

- help children understand that they have a role to play in supporting both the parent who is away and the one who is left behind

- help children understand that even though their parent is away they are still loved and remembered.

✦ Background

Many people now have jobs that take them away from home for extended periods of time. They may come back at weekends, or they may be away for longer – workers on foreign engineering contracts, for example, may be away from home for a long time, and then be back for an extended leave.

This lifestyle puts particular pressures on family life. The family miss the absent parent of course, but there is more to it than that. The family develops a routine of its own without the absent parent, and when the parent returns he or she may then feel like an outsider. The time that he or she needs to talk and catch up with things may not be easy for the rest of the family – continuing with their day to day lives – to accommodate.

Children are as much involved in this situation as adults. They will miss their parent and be glad to see him or her home, but will also need to continue with their everyday existence – 'Hi! Can't stop now, I've got to meet my friends…' This can seem quite hurtful to the returning parent.

This assembly deals not only with parental absence, but also with the pressures of their homecomings.

✦ Before the assembly

Optional Find out about the situation of any children who have experienced a parent working away from home. If possible, discuss the forthcoming assembly with the parent who is left at home and ask him or her to describe particular problems that they have to face and which they don't mind you using as part of the assembly.

📖 The assembly

All of you here – just like all of the other children in schools all over the country – have parents who do very different things. Some of your parents work and some of them don't. Of those who work, some work part-time and

Parents working away from home

some work full-time. Some work early in the morning and some work late at night. Some don't have to go far to work, and some have longer journeys. Work is so far away for some parents that it's hard for them to get there and back easily, so they have to stay away from home for a little while – a few days or a few weeks, even a few months.

* * * * * * * * * * * *

Optional I want to tell you about… *(tell the prepared story of the family in your school's own experience)*. Some others of you may have parents working away from home, too.

Or, if you haven't used the option
That might be the case for some of you.

* * * * * * * * * * * *

Now I'm sure you know why they have to work away from home. It's because that's where their job is, and because they want to do the job to provide a good home for you. If the job they were good at were round the corner, they would like it better and so would you, but, unfortunately, things don't always quite work out like that.

Here's a story about a family that spends some time apart.

* * * * * * * * * * * *

In the early mornings, Sarah usually lay awake and thought about her dad, working on an oil pipeline far away in the Middle East. She only had a vague idea what an oil pipeline was like. It was a big pipe that carried oil, presumably, but that was about it. She did know that it kept her dad away from home a lot. 'That

pipeline takes a lot of looking after,' her grandad had said once, and his words often came back into her mind. As she lay in bed in the mornings thinking about her dad, she would sometimes say it aloud to her teddy.

Sarah almost always thought about her dad when she first woke up. As the day went on, the thoughts about him tended to go away, because her life was so busy that there were lots of other things she had to think about. Once she got out of bed, everything seemed to happen at once. She had to get ready for school, have breakfast, and help her mum get her little brother sorted out for the child minder, as Mum had to do everything else and get herself ready for work.

Then at weekends there was shopping to be done and her grandparents to visit. And every Sunday her mum would say, 'Sarah, have you written to your dad this week?' Sometimes she had, but sometimes she would feel a bit guilty because she hadn't, especially if she had spoken to him on the phone.

There were times when Sarah really missed her dad though. She missed him when there were things that she was proud of, like netball matches. The other girls' families would all be around the court shouting and cheering, but her dad wasn't there. Often her mum wasn't there either, because life was so busy for her with Dad away. It didn't seem fair at times like that. And when there were any problems in school, her mum had to sort them out on her own, and that was difficult too, with her work and everything. Mum sometimes got tired and a bit ratty.

But mostly, they jogged along quite well when Dad was away – they had all slipped into a sort of routine. But still, it was always good when he came home.

Parents working away from home

Dad always arrived in a taxi from the airport. They never knew exactly when it would be, because sometimes the flights were delayed, or he had to spend a long time in the baggage area waiting for his suitcase. He wasn't always in the best of moods when he first arrived. 'He's sometimes a bit tetchy,' Sarah said to teddy. 'He wants us all to take notice of him, I think.'

Once, Dad had arrived just as Mum was going out to drop baby James at the childminder and go to work, and Sarah was going to school. Sarah lay in bed thinking about that visit, and wrinkled up her nose at the memory. Dad had been really annoyed. He had wanted everyone to stay behind and be with him.

'I've got to go to work!' Mum had said. 'Sarah has to go to school. Life can't stop just because you've arrived. We'll see you when we get in. There's food in the fridge. Do yourself a fry-up.'

Oh dear. That had been a bit of a row. What had Dad said? 'Is your work more important than me then? And can't Sarah stay off for an hour or two to see her dad?'

Mum had used one of her regular sayings, 'I can't stop to argue. We manage all the time without you, and our lives have to go on.'

'Right then!' Dad had replied. 'I'll catch the next plane back!'

Sarah had burst into tears at that point, and the row had got worse. Mum wouldn't even let baby James stay home with Dad.

'It's ages since you've seen him,' she had said. He won't know you properly, and you won't know how to manage when he needs anything. Stop being silly. Look, you've had a long flight. Have some breakfast and have a nap, and we'll be home when you wake up!'

Sarah picked up teddy and held him over her head so that she could speak to him more clearly. 'What a morning that was,' she said.

She had been a bit tearful when she got to school, and Miss Creasey, her teacher, had taken her on one side. She was a bit surprised when Sarah told her what the matter was.

Miss Creasey had said, 'I thought you were supposed to cry when someone went, not when they came back.'

'Well, it was all silly really,' replied Sarah.

Miss Creasey had thought for a while. 'You know,' she said, 'you have to see it from your dad's point of view. You've almost built a life without him, and that will sometimes make him feel as if he's not properly wanted, or needed. He can't even look after the baby. That must make him feel bad. And don't forget that he wants to see you all, too. He loves you very much and he misses you when he's away, just like you miss him. He just wants to come back and be able to spend time with you all.'

Sarah had nodded. Later that evening she had told her mum what she had talked about with Miss Creasey. Surprisingly, her mum knew exactly what Miss Creasey meant.

'I know it really, Sarah,' she had said. 'It's just that we carry on with the busy lives that we're used to, and Dad wants us to stop and give him some time, and to spend time with us. I know he gets lonely over there sometimes, when he thinks about us doing everything together here.

'I think it would help if we spent a bit more time writing to him when he's away, and making him feel part of what's going on. Perhaps, when there's a play or something going on at school, we can send him a programme, or ring him when we get in

Parents working away from home

afterwards, and tell him while it's still fresh in our minds. And if there's a problem, I'll ring him and ask for his opinion, instead of just getting on with sorting it out on my own.'

'I didn't like the argument,' said Sarah.

'Neither did any of us, Sarah,' Mum had said. 'If I'd stopped to think, we could have done something about it. He could have come with us, and dropped us all off. I could even have arranged to meet him at lunchtime. But I just couldn't slow down and think.'

'Having time for each other,' said Sarah.

'That's it,' said her mum. 'And that's easier when people are together all the time. But when they're not, they have to think about it a bit more carefully. We do all have things we can do. You could make sure that you write a letter to Dad every week so that he knows exactly what's going on here. You can tell him all about school and your friends and netball and gym club. And we could all make sure that we make time to sit and listen to him, when he wants to tell his stories about the Middle East, too. I could consult him more – the telephone's there after all, it's easy to talk to him. But I suppose what we really have to do, is try to slow down and think about each other. We're a good family, but we have to work at it if we want it to stay good.'

Pause.

● ● ● ● ● ● ● ● ● ● ●

For any of you who are in a situation like Sarah's, I want you to know that we all realise that it can be difficult for families when someone they love has to be away a lot of the time. It calls for a lot of understanding and patience from every member of the family, and that's not always easy. Sometimes the patience

runs out a little, and there are some tears, or even some anger.

But it's natural for that to happen – it shows that people care a lot for each other, if they get emotional about what's going on. If they didn't care, then they perhaps wouldn't get so worked up. But because they do, and because they love each other and miss each other, being separated is often hard.

☀ A prayer

God, be with all families, but especially those that have to be parted from each other because of the pressures of life. Bring understanding and patience to everyone, so that love will find a way to bridge the distances between them. Help us all, too, in our family and school lives, to think before we speak, and to remember the real needs of all the people around us. Amen.

☀ A thought

The playwright William Shakespeare said that 'parting is such sweet sorrow'. That's very true when you think about it. When someone you love goes away you feel sorrow, but you also know that they'll return and that's something sweet to look forward to. A person who's away is still in your thoughts and your heart, and you are still in theirs. The more you think of them and are considerate to them, the better and sweeter it will be when they come back.

Worries about tests and exams

✦ Introduction

Everyday classroom testing seldom causes problems for children, but when more formal exams come along, such as entrance examinations to secondary or upper school or national tests at Key Stage 2, then the issue can become a sensitive one. This assembly could be given either by individual classteachers or to the whole year group affected.

Aims:

The aims of this assembly are to

- help children to see that the test or examination they face may be difficult, but not impossible

- help children to see that it can be exciting to face a challenge, provided they are prepared for it.

✦ Background

Many children become worried when they are faced with an important test or examination. There may also be parental pressure to do well and the importance of results for an entrance exam to secondary school will be so great for some parents that their anxiety and concern is likely to be transferred to their child.

Equally, some schools will be worried over league tables and the results of national tests or some other LEA or Common Entrance type of exam and, again this anxiety may be transferred to the children.

Individual children who are nervous, and even frightened of the forthcoming tests, can, in an atmosphere of general worry, affect others too, and cause them also to feel anxious and unsure.

The challenge for the teacher is to give reassurance which is realistic and does not avoid the importance of the occasion, but which at the same time does not unsettle those children who are dealing with it well and staying relatively unaffected.

Do assess the level of anxiety with the staff before you give the assembly – there's no point in raising anxiety unnecessarily. You may decide that it is only necessary to do the assembly with some classes.

✦ Before the assembly

Think carefully about who is the best person to give the assembly. It may be the class teacher, or it may require the extra authority of the head of year or headteacher – your circumstances will dictate this decision.

Optional Write the four points on page 117 on an OHT or on the board.

📖 The assembly

'There's no such word as "can't".'

How many of you have heard someone say that? It's one of those things that adults say to children, isn't it?

Perhaps they say it to you when you whinge a bit and say *(put on a whiny voice)*, 'Mum, I can't do that!'

What does, 'There's no such word as "can't"' mean?

Worries about tests and exams

In one way it doesn't make sense, because there obviously is such a word, because it's there in the sentence. And people use it all the time.

'Sorry, I can't go shopping with you because I've got to mend my bike.'

'I can't get up in the mornings!'

'No, you can't stay up and watch *(a current post 9pm programme)*.'

In fact 'can't' isn't really the right word to use in these sorts of sentences.

You could go shopping and mend your bike later, but mending your bike is your priority. You could get up earlier – it's just not very easy! You could stay up to watch TV, it's just that your parent's won't let you.

But there really are some things you can't do. You can't fly by flapping your arms. You can't run at a hundred miles an hour. You can't get to Timbuctoo in five minutes. *(Take some examples from the children of things they can't do.)*

What people really mean when they say 'There's no such word as "can't"' is that there are things you think you can't do, and perhaps you could if you tried. We know you can't fly by flapping your arms, but if people had not tried ways to make it come true, then we would never have invented aeroplanes.

Suppose someone said to you, 'Here are two pencils and a sheet of paper. I want you to draw a horse with one hand and a cow with the other, both at the same time.' You might well say, 'I can't do that!' and you would probably be right.

Then I might say, 'There's no such word as "can't"', and encourage you to have a try. And suppose you kept on trying – you practised every day until your hands ached. You concentrated and concentrated and slowly you got better at it. Can you imagine that eventually you would be able to do it? I reckon that at least some of you could. You'd have learned to do something that seemed impossible.

So you see, when people say these things, they are really trying to encourage you. Sometimes they know you can do something, even though you have doubts about it.

There's a **test/exam, tomorrow/this week** *(as appropriate)*. No, don't pull faces, all those of you who did! And don't think you can't do the **test/exam**, because you can. In fact it is specially made so that you can do it. It's not like asking you to draw a horse and a cow at the same time. It's going to be about things you've learned here in school – not something you've never done before – so all of you can get most of it done.

Some of it will be hard of course, but then it wouldn't be worth doing if it was all easy. A **test/exam** is supposed to test you after all. But being hard is not the same as being impossible. You can do lots of hard things *(name some activities that take place in your school if appropriate, particularly ones which those who may be worried are involved in)*. This **test/exam** is just one other hard thing that you can do.

So I won't say, 'There's no such word as "can't".' But I will say, 'Hard doesn't mean impossible'. If we give you something that makes you think and work really hard, it

Worries about tests and exams

doesn't mean we think you can't do it. It means we think you can do it, and we'd rather test you on something challenging than on something easy.

So if you've been worrying about this **test/exam**, I want you to stop now. I know that it's not that easy though, so I'm going to give you four suggestions to help you stop worrying.

Optional *Show the prepared OHT, or write the following on the board*

- Take several deep, slow breaths before you begin, and every time you begin to feel a bit nervous or tense.

- Concentrate and try your hardest.

- Don't waste time when you're doing the **test/exam**.

- Remember this **test/exam** is only part of your work and no one is going to judge you on one test only.

Let's think together about this. We don't want easy things to do all the time. Life would be boring if there were no hard pieces of music to play, no hard matches, no hard books to read, no hard work to do in school. What's important is that we feel we can do the hard things if we try. We thrive on challenges and tests. We have to trust the people who set them to make them hard – so that we are challenged and so that we have the chance to be proud of ourselves – but not impossible.

☀ A prayer

Dear God, Help us not to worry about the **test/exam** that we are going to do. We know that we can only do our best and that worrying about it won't help us to answer the questions any better. Help us to answer them as best we can, so that we can be proud of ourselves and so that our families and friends can be proud of us too. Amen.

☀ A thought

All you can do is do your best, and as long as you do that there is no reason to worry. In any case worrying won't help you to answer the questions any better! If you don't worry, and do your best, then you know you can be proud of yourself when you have finished, and your families and friends can be proud of you too.

Coping with grief

✦ Introduction

This assembly considers the feelings that are caused by grief. You could use it, with some discretion, for example, when a grandparent has died and there are children or other close relatives in school. The assembly requires little preparation.

Aims:

The aims of this assembly are to

- help those in the assembly recognise that grief is an emotion they might experience

- confirm that grief is a well-known human feeling

- put a name to the feeling of grief

- describe the different ways in which adults express grief

- confirm that a wide range of expressions is acceptable.

✦ Background

During the primary school years, children's awareness of, and attitude to death changes. A young child may not actually understand the finality of death. He or she may have to be told several times that the lost person will not be coming back.

A young child may also feel guilty, believing that the death is in some way connected with his or her own behaviour. Children can become very curious about the nature of death and of dead bodies.

Older children may be intellectually capable of realising that death is final and permanent –

although acceptance of this may lead them to think about their own mortality.

Children will express their grief in different ways. One may cling to a family member and be reluctant to leave them. Another may appear to be relatively unaffected, though it would be a big mistake to take this at face value. Most mature adults know what grief is, and have a range of different words and actions with which to express it. But not all adults are good at expressing their grief and any changes in adult behaviour can have quite serious effects on young children.

Children may not even know the word 'grief'. They certainly experience it, but it comes as a set of powerful, previously unknown and highly distressing feelings that are difficult to bear and to express. Even very young children are capable of masking their feelings because they are afraid of adding to the more obvious distress of another family member.

(There are further notes on bereavement in Appendix 2, page 146, and organisations from which you can get further help and advice are listed under Appendix 3, Bereavement on page 150.)

Much of the help we can give to specific children at a time of real distress will be private or in small groups. This assembly might be used in a class group.

Coping with grief

✦ Before the assembly

This is a general assembly about grief to be used at a time when someone in school is either absent, because of a recent bereavement in their family, or obviously suffering as a result of such a bereavement. The assembly does not focus on any one child or adult in your school. Nevertheless, if you use it at a time of bereavement in school it is a good idea to talk with the bereaved adult, child or family first to let them know that you are going to give this assembly, both to support them and to help others realise how they are feeling.

📖 The assembly

I want to talk to you this morning about what happens when someone close to us dies. I don't want to talk about what happens to the person who has died. I'm going to talk about what happens to the people left behind.

We all know that everyone is born and everyone dies. It's one of the things we can't change in the world. But, however much we know this fact, it doesn't seem to help when someone close to us passes away. In many ways the feelings we have at this time are difficult to describe. Listen to what someone said recently. The person who is speaking is about my age – grown up with a job and lots of responsibilities.

When my dad died the first thing I remember was a feeling of being exhausted all of a sudden. I was just tired out. I hardly had any energy to move.

Then I remember feeling very flat. I didn't cry, which surprised me. I had expected to burst into tears as soon as I heard my dad had died, but I didn't. I just sat there feeling very empty. Nothing seemed to be in my head. Just a feeling of total emptiness.

That night a friend came round to see me. At one point she said something funny and I burst out laughing. I hadn't laughed for a few days. You might think that laughing would have made me feel better, but it didn't. I felt guilty that I was laughing so soon after my dad had died. Somehow, laughing made me feel worse.

In the next few days, there was so much to do that I didn't really have time to think about anything. And then one afternoon, shortly after the funeral was over, I cried for about two hours non-stop. And I didn't just cry, I howled and howled. Nothing could stop me crying and sobbing. For a couple of months after that I would suddenly start crying, without knowing it was going to happen. In a shop, talking pleasantly to a shop assistant, I would burst into tears with absolutely no warning. And then just as suddenly I would stop. I had no control over it at all.

I remember one other thing as well.

For a while I became quite horrible to my friends and family. I didn't mean to, of course, but I couldn't stop that either. All of a sudden I would get cross for no reason. Or I would promise to go out somewhere and then refuse at the last moment. It didn't happen all of the time, but it happened quite a lot. Sometimes my family didn't know what to do or say to me. It must have been quite horrible for them.

This lasted for two or three months. Eventually, I sort of started to return to normal, although even now – nearly a year later – I can still stand at the sink on a

Coping with grief

Saturday morning and suddenly cry for ten minutes without warning. And, of course, I still miss my dad.

Pause.

The strange mix of jumbled up feelings that the man was talking about is called grief. Grief is the special feeling we have when someone close to us dies. There are no rules to grief – we all show it in different ways. But grief usually makes us a different sort of person for a short while. Grief takes over our normal lives. It helps a great deal to have the support and understanding of those who love us – even if we are not always able to say thank you in the way we might want.

If you know someone who is grieving, then try your best to give your support. Try to understand what they are going through. If they behave strangely for a while, then be patient. All they are doing is grieving – and grieving is just as natural and normal as birth and death.

Optional *You could light a candle at this point to focus attention.*

A prayer

Dear God, help us to remember everyone who is sad and filled with grief. Many of us know what that feels like, so we understand. Please give them strength, and help us all to be thoughtful and to give our support. Amen.

A thought

Let's think about those people who are sad and filled with grief at this moment. Many of us know what that feels like, so we understand. Let us all be thoughtful and give those people our support.

I don't like my body

✦ Introduction

Children are increasingly conscious of their physical appearance, and the age at which this concern shows itself lowers all the time. As a result, primary schools are dealing with two connected problems – the early appearance of eating disorders, and the bullying and isolation of children who don't fit the image. The main victims are overweight children who may be bullied either physically or by name calling – but it's also true that children who are naturally very thin can also be called names or bullied.

Aims:

The aim of the assembly is to help children towards greater acceptance of their own bodies and to be less judgmental of personal appearance in others.

✦ Background

This is clearly a difficult area. You need to be aware of the risks of drawing attention to the problem you are trying to solve. At the same time, as with drug education for older children, there are times when ignoring an issue isn't an acceptable option. If you're aware that young children are talking to each other about slimming and dieting, or if it's clear that overweight or very thin children are being made miserable, then you need to take action. Much of what you do, of course, will be at an individual or class level in PSHE, and will be done with the advice and support of parents, health advisors, and the educational psychologist. (Professional help is particularly important when you become aware of a child with an eating disorder.) Assembly, as always,

provides an opportunity for asserting your school's values and beliefs about the way people should think of themselves and others.

* * *

Health educators estimate that 40 per cent of nine year olds have dieted, and some children as young as five or six are known to express the desire to be slim. Actual eating disorders also appear among primary children, though cases still seem to be rare (although it is difficult to be confident about issues like this.)

* * *

There's little mystery about why this should be. A generation obsessed with physical appearance and the ideal body is having children of its own. These children are brought up among people who are constantly dieting and talking about food in anxious, negative terms. Unsurprisingly, some families develop similar anxieties about their own children's appearance.

More subtly, where there's tension in a home, or actual abuse, a child may become food-obsessed because it's one aspect of life that he or she feels able to control.

* * *

An assembly can't deal with these background aspects directly. What it can do is reassure children that there really is such a thing as unconditional love, and that it is not acceptable to reject someone on the grounds of personal

I don't like my body • page 1 of 4

I don't like my body

appearance. In the same way, it's OK to like yourself the way you are, and there's no need to be angry or disappointed with the way you are.

✦ Before the assembly

As always, discuss with colleagues what you are going to do in this assembly, and why. The assembly tackles the subject by telling, in straightforward terms, the story of an older girl who starts to have eating problems because she feels she's overweight. It deliberately doesn't preach to the primary age group. The children are left to make the connection for themselves. The story is designed simply to state basic values – it's OK to like your body, and the people who love you do so unconditionally – your shape isn't an issue in that.

📖 The assembly

Anybody in your house slimming? I thought so. There is in our house, too. Sometimes I think everybody's slimming all the time. I think that's not always a good thing. It depends why they're doing it. If they think it will make them more healthy, or because the doctor's told them to do it, then that's probably OK. But if they think it will make people like them more, then that's a mistake, isn't it? We all know that we like people for what they are, not for what they look like. Let me tell you a story about somebody who made that very mistake. Better still, I'll read the story to you as she told it herself in her own words.

I'm Joanna. I'm a happily married woman now, with two lovely daughters, Amy and Michelle. They're both at primary school. Amy's nine and Michelle's seven.

I wasn't always married, of course, and I wasn't always happy. You know people think that teenagers are carefree and full of fun. But I wasn't full of fun at all. I was quite miserable when I was seventeen. And the reason was that I thought I was too fat. I used to look at myself in the mirror and think, 'Crikey, Joanna, you're gross!'

Sometimes I said it to my mum. I'd say, 'Mum, I'm far too fat. No boy will look at me like this. I look terrible.'

And my mum would look back at me and shake her head. She'd say, 'Joanna! I don't know what you are talking about. You look fine to me. I don't see what the problem is.'

And I would sulk, and think to myself, 'What do you know about it Mum? You're not me, are you?'

Then I'd go up to my room and look in the mirror again and shake my head.

When I first went to college I used to think that everyone was making fun of me behind my back. Looking back now, I don't think they were. In any case, I worried so much that I missed what was really important. What was really important was that I had a group of two or three really good friends. They liked me and I liked them. We talked about things together, and they never once said I was too fat. And I never commented on their appearance. In fact now I come to think of it all these years later, I can't remember too well whether they were fat or thin. I just remember what they were

I don't like my body

actually like – there was Jackie who was really funny, and there was Maxine who couldn't spell, but used to laugh about it, and there was Gloria who was always a hit with the lads, and Ramandeep who was always bringing us biscuits from her dad's shop. I remember their faces, and the things they said, and the tricks we got up to when we wanted to annoy the lecturers at college.

Those are the good memories. But I hadn't been at college long before the bad time started. What happened was that I got really hung up on the idea that I was fat. I started to try to slim. I wouldn't eat my lunch at college – I would get the sandwiches my mum had put in my lunchbox and put them in the bin. I might eat an apple, but nothing else. Then at home I'd play about with my tea and say I wasn't hungry.

My mum started to get worried about me. She said I was going to make myself ill. But I was convinced I was still fat and I'd look at myself in the mirror and hate what I saw.

Even my friends worried about me. They used to say that I was looking bad. I felt bad, too. I got that I wouldn't go out. I'd say to my mum that I couldn't go out, and I wouldn't tell her why. And all the time I still thought I looked much too overweight.

My mum was worried to death – she told me that later. She tried to tempt me with the lovely things she used to make – beautiful chips, and lovely puddings. But I would just push them away and say I wasn't hungry.

It was a miserable time, and all because for some reason that I still don't understand, I didn't like my own body. Can you imagine that? I didn't like my own body. Even though my real friends didn't really see it – they saw me, just as I saw them.

I know now that I could have died. Some people have died from being too worried about their weight, and not eating properly. I was lucky to escape before things got too serious. I came through it because people loved me and cared for me.

I've discovered since that quite a lot of people have that sort of trouble. It's not their own fault really – I was a bit relieved when I found that out. It's often because of other worries and troubles that they have in their minds, sometimes without even knowing. But it does help if people know that they are loved for who they are. And other people help by not making comments on anyone's appearance. Good friends help by concentrating on what the real person is like.

I have to get my daughters' tea ready now. I think they'll enjoy it, they usually do. What's that? Are they slim or overweight? What a question to ask. They're my lovely daughters. I love them dearly and they love me. That's what matters.

© **pfp** 2002 ISBN 1 874050 57 0   May be photocopied for use only within the purchasing institution **pfp**, 61 Gray's Inn Road, London WC1X 8TH
I don't like my body • page 3 of 4   **123**

I don't like my body

☀ A prayer

Lord, we thank you for our bodies. We thank you that we are all different from each other. And we ask you to help us appreciate our friends, and ourselves, for what we're really like inside.

Help all people who have worries about their appearance to know that they are loved, and give us the ability to show the love that we have for our friends and relatives. Amen.

☀ A thought

The Christian Bible says, 'love your neighbour as yourself.' That's a very good idea. But the first thing you have to do is love yourself – not by being selfish or vain, but by being comfortable with the way you are. If you're comfortable with the way you are, you'll be comfortable with other people and they'll be fine with you.

Facial disfigurement

✦ Introduction

This assembly is about facial disfigurement. It's at the lower end of primary school that children who are born with disfigurement may first really encounter the reactions of others, though they may have been aware of glances and even remarks when they've been out shopping.

Aims:

The aims of the assembly are to

- prepare children for the arrival of a fellow pupil with facial disfigurement

- help children with disfigurement to cope with school

- support policies aimed at heading off any bullying or name calling.

✦ Background

One child in five hundred is seriously affected by a facial disfigurement, either genetic (such as strawberry birth mark, or neurofibramatosis) or caused by an accident (eg. burns and dog). A smaller number – about one in a hundred – has a feature that's not so serious but is noticeable (such as a smaller birth mark, repaired cleft lip and palate).

This means that just about every teacher who's in the profession for a few years is going to encounter a child with a facial disfigurement. In mainstream schools, though, it's still going to be unusual enough for the teacher to need some help in knowing how to cope with the difficulties that can arise both for the child and for the other children.

Here are some general principles to bear in mind.

Don't assume that you'll be able to say 'just ignore it'. A facial difference demands attention – it's built into us to focus in on people's faces. So you, the child, the parents and other children need to be ready with the right response.

You'll be filled with inner questions about the condition itself – what is it? Does it hurt? Will it get better? But as a teacher your concern is with the child and how the condition affects learning, social skills and development.

The child's parents have an entirely different set of experiences from those of other parents. They may have had many wearying and distressing times with hospitals and consultants, with high hopes and disappointments. They have had to cope all the time with other people's reactions, including those of other family members. Their other children's lives may have been affected by the attention given to the disfigured child. If there's been an accident, there may be guilt and recrimination. You will probably never know the details of all this, but there may come a time when you need to try to understand why parents are reacting in a particular way.

• • • • • • • • • • • •

For all those reasons, when you do an assembly or any other activity that focuses directly or indirectly on the child with disfigurement, you must talk to the parents first.

Our assembly provides a case study (based on real life) and some things to say that may make life better for any disfigured child in your school.

Facial disfigurement

✦ Before the assembly

What you do before the assembly, and how you handle the assembly itself depends on your precise aim – whether it's to prepare children for the arrival of a disfigured child, or whether it's to tackle issues that come up while the child is in school. If the child is already in school, then it's possible that he or she may be able to take part in the assembly. If the child does want to take part, as one of those who talks about their physical features, the assembly will be even more powerful. Secondary school and older primary children may feel able to take part. But don't push this, and always work with the child's parents.

Even if you're not going to ask the child to take part or even be present, you should talk to the parents of the child. And if the child is already in school, talk to the child also. Explain why you want to do this. Draw out from him or her what ought to be achieved.

📖 The assembly

There are thousands of millions of people in the world. That's a number that's difficult to imagine, so let me take another one. If you draw a very, very big circle around our school you'll probably find that about twenty thousand people live inside that circle. That's about as many as you'd get at a really good league soccer match – a medium sized stadium full if you like.

Now, suppose all these people were standing in a long line – maybe queuing up to get into the stadium. And suppose that among these people were about ten people that you know – members of your family. I know that you could walk quickly along that very long line of people and pick out those ten people. You could, couldn't you? It wouldn't be difficult.

I'd go a bit further than that. I reckon that if all the thousands of millions of people in the whole world lined up in a great long line, you could go along and pick out your ten friends. That's if you had time to walk along such a long line. You could do that, couldn't you?

Let me ask you why you could do that? Why can you pick out your ten friends from among all those thousands of other people?

It's obvious, isn't it? It's because you can recognise them. And why can you recognise them? Because they look different from the people around them. And why do they look different from the people around them? Because we're all different from each other. Every single one of us – every last one of all the millions and millions on the earth – is different from everyone else – so different that we can always recognise the people we know, no matter where we see them and no matter how many other people are around.

Let's look at some of those differences.

(Get ten children you know well out to the front. If the child with the disfigurement has agreed to take part, treat them like the others.)

Now, let's see if each of these people can tell us one thing about themselves that's different from the other nine. It might be hair colour, or the shape of the nose – anything at all.

(Encourage the children to do this.)

Now, I'll tell you something else. We all have something about ourselves that we don't like very much. One person may be fed up with her hair, another may not like the shape of his nose. Sometimes we think everyone's looking. And maybe sometimes they are. Let me tell you a little story.

Facial disfigurement

Let me tell you about Ralph. Now Ralph was a happy lad, but rather lonely in many ways because he hadn't got any brothers and sisters, so he was quiet and he did a lot of reading. He wore glasses, and sometimes he got called specky or four eyes at school, but he didn't mind that much because his glasses helped him to see, and that's what was important.

Then when he was about eleven, his teacher asked everyone in the class to draw pictures of themselves. Ralph drew himself from the side. Now he'd never really drawn himself from the side, so he did his best, and drew this normal looking lad with glasses and an ordinary nose and mouth and chin.

When he'd finished, the boy sitting next to him looked at the picture and said, 'Ralph! Is that what you think you look like?'

Ralph was a bit taken aback, and he said, 'Not really,' because he didn't want to look stupid. But he thought to himself that maybe he didn't look like that from the side at all.

So that evening at home, he went into the bathroom and got his dad's shaving mirror and did some manoeuvring with the shaving mirror and the main bathroom mirror until he could see himself from the side, which he'd never seen before.

And Ralph got quite a shock. Because he didn't like what he saw at all. He thought he looked quite different from what he expected. He could see that his teeth were sticking out, and he had a big nose. It all came as the kind of surprise that he didn't want. Suddenly he realised why some of the other children pulled faces at him and stuck their teeth out on purpose to make fun of him.

It took Ralph a long time to get over seeing himself like that. He started to think of himself as ugly, and he lost a lot of confidence in

himself. As he got older he didn't like talking to girls because he believed that they always thought of him as ugly, and didn't take him seriously.

Eventually, Ralph got over the feeling of not liking his appearance, but it took him a very long time. What made him feel better in the end was the gradual realisation that he had many good friends who liked him for what was inside – a good sense of humour and a kind nature. It wasn't until he met a girl who loved him for what he was and married him that he was really cured of his self consciousness.

You see, it's what's inside that matters. Faces change. Hair changes colour. Sometimes it disappears altogether! People start to wear glasses, or walk differently from when they were younger. What's outside changes, but what's inside is what's true about you. Now I'm going to go along these ten people and tell you what I see when I look at them.

(Go to each of the ten and say something positive about their personality and behaviour.)

What matters, you see, is what's inside. I look at each one of you and I recognise you because I know what you look like. And you recognise me because you know what I look like. But I don't look for long at what's on the outside. I think to myself, 'That's so and so, who got a headteacher's award yesterday.' Or I think, 'That's whatshername, who played so well at netball last Saturday.' Or I think, 'That's the helpful boy who helped me bring my things in from the car this morning.' Those are the things that I see, and those are the things that matter.

Facial disfigurement

☀ A prayer

Lord, we believe that we are all made in your
image, and that you love every one of us for
what we are. You do not look at the outside,
you see the beauty that's inside. Help us to see
each other as you see us. More importantly,
help us to see ourselves as you see us –
beautiful human beings, made in your image,
filled with kindness and good humour. Amen.

☀ A thought

Sometimes, when a person says something
funny, their friend will laugh and say, 'What
are you like, eh?' It's a very true remark,
because the joke, or the remark that makes
people laugh, or feel good – that's what you
are like.

Understanding mental illness

✦ Introduction

Many children know someone who is mentally ill and may have a mentally ill person in their immediate family. This assembly is aimed at giving some small measure of support to children who have a mentally ill person living with them and at the wider school population who may be making fun of the mentally ill. It requires some brief preparation – see 'Before the assembly' below.

Aims:

The aims of the assembly are to

- inform children about mental illness

- help provide quiet support to children who are living with mental illness.

✦ Background

Anxiety and fear are likely to be the strong emotional response from children who have a parent or sibling suffering from mental illness. Their lives can be subject to periods when things are reasonably normal and then periods when there is crisis and even trauma. All of this can and usually does affect their behaviour and progress in school. The taunts and jibes of other pupils can be particularly distressing, and this assembly can be a way of talking about such issues without putting the spotlight on a particular child.

• • • • • • • • • • • •

If you are using this assembly as a response to a particular child's situation, you might choose to do it when the child is out of school for some reason, so as not to make him or her feel uncomfortable. Be careful to speak generally, rather than referring to any specific situations.

(There is a list of further resources and organisations in Appendix 3, Mental health on page 154.)

✦ Before the assembly

You will need

- the supplied OHT master (see page 133)

- an overhead projector

- a working computer (if you have a data projector, so much the better).

• •

📖 The assembly

Show the OHT.

This person has something wrong with her. What do you think the problem is?

That's right. She's broken her leg. You know our bodies can often have things go wrong with them, just as something can go wrong with a bike or a car. Things break, or stop working, and you have to get them put right.

Let's think about someone who has a broken leg. Has anyone here had a broken leg? Not at all funny, is it? It hurts when you do it, and then it's uncomfortable, because you have to wear a plastercast and have to keep going back to the hospital to get it checked. Luckily, though, it always heals up, especially when you're young. Older people's bones take a bit longer to heal, but even with old people, a break can usually be sorted out.

Understanding mental illness

While your leg is broken, it won't do what it's supposed to do. You can't put your weight on it – not easily, anyway. And you can't run, jump, or even walk properly, or do any of the things you can do when your leg is in one piece.

You look at your leg and your brain says 'Leg! Start walking!' But it takes no notice, because it can't do what your brain is telling it to do.

Now, think about another person. He has something wrong with him, too. But we can't see it. This is Ray, and he has a mental illness – something wrong inside his brain. A lot of the time he's quite OK, but sometimes things seem to go wrong and he starts getting the wrong messages from his brain. He thinks that everyone is talking about him even when they're not, and he gets angry and afraid. And sometimes he goes off on his own for long periods because he thinks that's what he has to do. When he does that everyone gets worried about him.

Raymond has a loving family who are very concerned about him. They help him as much as they can – they make sure he keeps his hospital appointments and they make sure he takes his medicine, because his medicine helps him when he's going through a bad patch of being angry and frightened. It's difficult to understand what happens to Ray. It might help if we think about this computer.

Point to the computer.

Now, look at this computer. I can type on the keyboard, and words come up on the screen. This cable is taking messages from the keyboard into the computer, and it is then changing the messages into text on the screen.

If I had the right kind of computer, it could speak those words to me. If I had a printer connected, it could print them out. The keyboard doesn't work it all out, any more than the printer does. It all happens inside here. *(Tap the computer.)*

So if it goes wrong in here, what might happen?

Well, perhaps the screen might go blank, and nothing would happen at all. I could type away and there would be nothing. Or perhaps it would scramble the messages, so that even if I typed real words, words that don't exist would come up on the screen or out of the printer. The computer may have picked up a virus that makes things appear on the screen that I haven't put there. That's really weird, but it can happen.

If there's something wrong in here *(tap the computer)*, everything else does the wrong things.

So the computer is a bit like our brains. It makes everything else work – it's the central processor.

And, very occasionally, the same sort of thing happens to a person's brain as happens to a computer. It gets ill, and scrambled messages start going in and out. Perhaps messages that aren't really there.

That can happen to all of us sometimes – we think we've heard something, or we think we have seen something out of the corner of our eye, but it wasn't really there. That's quite normal, just as it's quite normal for a computer to do strange things occasionally. Sometimes, though, it's more serious. A person becomes mentally ill, like Ray, and the brain really mixes things up.

Understanding mental illness

For example, one of the things that happens to Ray is that he hears voices that aren't really there. He's not making it up, because he really does hear the voices. And they tell him to do things – when he goes off on his own, it's because the voices in his head have told him to do it.

Something like that can ruin your whole life. It can make a mentally ill person really miserable.

And it's no good going up to the person and saying, 'Don't worry. The voices aren't really there,' because to the ill person the voices actually are there, just as the wrong words on the screen of the faulty computer are really there, even if they weren't typed in.

It's not just hearing voices, of course – there are lots of other ways in which the brain can go wrong. A person may feel afraid and distressed all the time, for no real reason.

You feel as if you want to say, 'Cheer up! There's nothing really wrong!' But it's no good saying that, because to the ill person the fear is very real. There is something wrong, and a few kind words won't take it away.

• • • • • • • • • • •

Mental illness is real. It is wrong connections and faulty workings in the brain. It causes great unhappiness to the person who is ill. And also very great unhappiness to whoever loves that person, or is trying to look after them.

But can a mentally ill person get better? Can the brain be mended, like your broken leg, or the broken computer?

Well, yes it can, although it's not as simple as that. The brain is a tremendously complicated organ, and nobody really understands all of its workings. So curing mental illness can be

difficult and doesn't always work completely. But there are medicines that can help a lot, and it can help to have a stay in hospital. Ray has taken a lot of medicine, and been in and out of hospital at various times.

What matters with Ray, though, is that his family love him and want to care for him. His mum and dad, and his younger brother are patient and understanding with him when he gets angry. It's not easy – sometimes Ray is really difficult to live with. And I have to say it doesn't help when local children shout things at him and laugh at him because he behaves in ways they don't understand. I know you wouldn't do that.

So Ray's family and close friends do their best, and Ray's doctor and the hospital will help when things get really bad.

• • • • • • • • • •

(Show the OHT of the person with the broken leg again.) Remember, you wouldn't ask this poor patient to run round the playground, so we can't ask someone like Ray just to cheer up and do things they just can't do. They need our help and understanding.

Understanding mental illness

☀ **A prayer**

Dear God, we know there are many kinds of
illness. We know that illnesses of the brain can
be very upsetting for the people who suffer and
for the people near to them. Give comfort to
mentally ill people, and courage to their
families, and knowledge and skill to their
doctors. And give understanding and
compassion to all of us. Amen.

☀ **A thought**

There are many kinds of illness. Usually when
people have sick bodies they are treated kindly
and given support, but people who are
mentally ill sometimes get treated unkindly
instead. If we know anyone who has a mental
illness, we will try and be more understanding
about their problems, and try to help them,
and their families who are looking after them,
as much as we can.

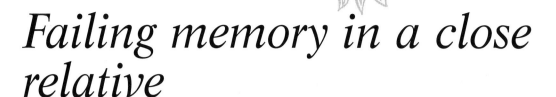

Failing memory in a close relative

✦ Introduction

This assembly uses a story about a grandparent with Alzheimer's Disease to get children to reflect about the illnesses and infirmities of old age. It requires some brief preparation – see 'Before the assembly' below.

Aims:

The aims of this assembly are to

- explain some of the facts about ageing

- give reassurance that all the love and care given in the past cannot be wiped out

- show that a new relationship, with changed responsibilities, might be possible.

✦ Background

Many children have special relationships with grandparents, or with other older relatives and friends, and it can be both distressing and frightening if the passing years cause these people to become ill and behave in unfamiliar ways. If there is a personality change, for example, caused by memory loss or anxiety about terminal illness, then the effect on a child may be more severe than parents and teachers suspect. This assembly is not only meant to reassure the child, but also to show him or her that you do understand and that you can support him or her.

(There is a list of further resources and organisations in Appendix 3, Alzheimer's Disease on page 158.)

✦ Before the assembly

Make some discreet enquiries among the staff to see if any of them have personal experience of Alzheimer's or similar diseases in their family. Make sure that the assembly theme won't be upsetting for them.

If they do have such experience, they might even wish to contribute to the discussion of this issue by talking about their own experiences at a follow-up assembly, or to a class group.

📖 The assembly

One of the best things about family life is the way that people of different ages can enjoy being together.

I bet lots of you have had new babies coming into your family. Those of you who are old enough to remember when your little brother or sister was born, will remember how everybody makes a fuss of a baby. Your parents, your aunts and uncles, your grandparents, you – I bet everyone, of all ages in your family, got together around the baby and made a fuss. And I bet the baby really enjoyed it too!

But then, the little baby will grow first into a toddler and then into a pupil in the nursery, able to talk and do lots of things. Everyone will still enjoy being with **him/her** but their relationships will be different. And they will be different too depending on who the person is – whether it's a sister, an aunt or a gran.

© **pfp** 2002 ISBN 1 874050 57 0 May be photocopied for use only within the purchasing institution **pfp**, 61 Gray's Inn Road, London WC1X 8TH

Failing memory in a close relative

Adults don't usually make quite as much fuss over children as they do over brand new babies, but they still like spending time with them very much.

Adults like to introduce children to the things that they like doing – fishing, going to watch sport, reading books, singing in choirs, playing instruments. Adults really love introducing younger people to the things they have enjoyed all their lives, and then watching the young person enjoy it too.

And then there are the much older people in the family – grandparents, or great grandparents. They can't get around as much as they did perhaps, so they might not take children out to do lots of active things. But instead they often like to sit and talk with, or watch, younger people, and the younger people like to look after them and bring them things to see. How many of you have said, 'Look at this, Gran!' in the last few days?

And just as babies change as they grow into children, so do the other members of the family as they grow older. You might know from your own experience that families don't stay the same. The older sister who used to play with you, and help you, starts to go out with her friends more. Then perhaps she may move away, to go to college perhaps, or because of her job. Perhaps, then, she'll get married and have children of her own.

And by that point you'll be older and different too. You'll still enjoy being with her, and feel proud of her, but the relationship you have with her will be different, because you'll both have got older and changed.

And as older people grow older still, our relationship with them may change again. They may grow quieter, and less active. And sometimes they may fall ill and be less

interested in what other people are doing. That doesn't always happen, but when it does, we have to remember that we can still love them and that even though they may not say much, they may now need you just as you used to need them.

● ● ● ● ● ● ● ● ● ● ●

Listen to this story.

John didn't want to go to the nursing home. 'Why do I have to go?' he said. 'I don't like it there. I don't like the people there and it's boring.'

His dad got annoyed. 'John, don't argue. You're going and that's it. Your grandad likes to see you.'

'No, he doesn't!' said John. 'He doesn't even know whether I'm there or not. He just sits there in his chair.'

John's mum decided to chip in, because she could see that his dad was about to get really angry. She had an idea.

'John, come in the living room a minute.'

She made him sit down, and she went over to the bookshelf and got out one of her photograph albums. 'Let's look at this for a minute or two.'

She sat down beside John, and opened it up. John liked looking through the old photographs. His mum had albums that went back to before he was born, and he liked looking at the photographs of his dad in silly trousers. His dad always tried to tell him they were fashionable in those days, but really they just looked silly.

His mum turned to a photograph taken at the seaside some years before. There was John,

Failing memory in a close relative

looking very small – about five years old – and his mum and dad, and his grandad, all together, laughing on the prom.

'Remember that?' asked his mum. John nodded. 'Blackpool. We went to see the illuminations. Grandad took me on the Big Dipper.'

'Dad had the time of his life,' said his mum. 'It was a year after Gran died, and he'd come to live with us. That holiday was the first time I'd seen him really cheerful, for ages. We hardly saw you two – he took you off to the beach, on the trams, on the Pleasure Beach. You were inseparable. And it stayed that way for ages didn't it?'

John nodded.

His mum went on. 'He took you fishing. He even took you to the male voice choir rehearsal. His dream was that you'd join the choir one day, and stand beside him. He used to talk about it a lot. I think he knew he'd be too old, though, by the time you were old enough to join. You loved your grandad didn't you?'

John nodded again.

'So do you love him now?'

'Well,' said John. 'He's not the same is he? He doesn't know me any more. And it's not like it used to be.'

'Nothing is like it used to be,' said his mum. 'Look at the photographs. Your dad and me have changed. You've changed. Your grandad can't do the things he used to do. He can't even look after himself any more. And we don't know whether he knows us or not, really. We go and talk to him, and try to show him that we love him, and we have to trust that somewhere inside himself he can hear that and understand it. Love's a powerful thing, you

know. It can get through when other feelings can't.'

John nodded again.

'Still nodding, John?' asked his mum, laughing. 'Are you coming to the nursing home? Tell you what. You can do some of the talking this time. Tell him how much you enjoyed yourself when you were at Blackpool that time, and when you went fishing. He may not seem to hear, but I reckon if he hears anyone, he'll hear you. He was good to you then, and he needs you now.'

John nodded yet again, and stood up ready to go to the nursing home.

Pause.

* * * * * * * * * * *

Most of the illnesses that we have don't really change us. We are ill, and perhaps a bit grumpy for a little while, but then we get better and go back to being our normal selves.

But some of the illnesses that people get when they are older are not like that. Some older people do change when they are ill, and they stop being quite the same person that they were before.

This sort of thing can often be difficult for families to cope with. Sometimes it's a little strange, sometimes it's upsetting and perhaps a little frightening, and sometimes, if we're honest – and especially for children – it's a little boring. You've got lots of energy and want to do things that that person can't do any more.

But in these cases it's important for us to remember some things.

Failing memory in a close relative

If we are a little frightened, because the person seems so different, we must remind ourselves that they are ill, and that it is the illness that has made them change. And then we must remember that someone who's ill is not someone to be frightened of, they are someone who needs to be treated with kindness and understanding.

And we must also remember the person as they were before they became ill, too. If we remember all the good times we have had with them, and all the special things about them, then it makes it easy to carry on loving them, as we have always done, and giving them the kindness and understanding that they need.

Let's finish with a **prayer/special thought** about that.

 ## A prayer

Dear God, help us to understand what it is like to be old, and help us to be thoughtful and patient with old people who are ill and who forget things. Let us remember that they are not different people inside, and remember all the things they have done and what they were like before. Let us remember the love that we can share with them and that they need our love and kindness more than ever before. Amen.

A thought

Let's think about how life can change for a while.

Things can never stay the same can they? Babies grow up. Young people become adults. Adults grow older. Sometimes our friends change – people we depended on start to depend on us. People we used to look after start to look after us. The relationships are still good – love survives – but they work in different ways. And when someone falls ill, or starts to forget things, or seems not to know things any more, we can remember that they are still the same person really, and that they need our love even more than before.

Friends moving away

✦ Introduction

This assembly is to use when parting is an issue for some of the children – particularly when a popular family is moving away, or there is evidence of a child being upset by a parting. Or it can be part of the normal assembly programme. It requires some brief preparation – see 'Before the assembly' below.

Aims:

The aims of this assembly are to

- let children know that the school recognises the pain they are feeling at parting with a good friend

- point out that the parting of friends is something that happens in life.

✦ Background

Young children can make friendships which are so close that parting is like a sort of bereavement. This is partly because children do not have the experience which enables an adult to accept that people will come and go, in and out of their lives, that even very close relationships can be temporary, and that a 'best friend' might go away for ever.

This is a situation that can happen for any number of reasons, and it will, of course, depend on your particular situation whether you feel it is appropriate to cover, in an assembly – you won't want to run the risk of upsetting or 'spotlighting' the friends left behind. If a well-known child has left, however, you may wish to use this assembly a week or two after they have gone as a way of discussing the feelings that children will be having.

✦ Before the assembly

Gather the names of some pupils who have friends from whom they have been parted. Include staff if you like. Discuss with them the theme of the forthcoming assembly.

📖 The assembly

Walk in to assembly, after the children if possible. As you enter, call 'Goodbye' through the door, and wave as though you are leaving someone. Then turn round, and greet the children with a big smile and a 'Hello'.

Meeting and parting. We do it all the time. Each morning we meet our friends in school – I've seen many of you rush up to talk to each other in the playground or call out to each other as soon as you're near enough to be heard. And just before all these meetings you probably had a parting, when you said goodbye to everyone at home. Then later on we part from our friends at school and then we meet again with our families at home.

So meeting and parting are part of everyone's lives.

But some meetings and partings are not so frequent. Perhaps we see some people just once a week, or even once a year on special occasions.

It's good to meet, but in a way that's like one side of a coin. Every coin has two sides. Good to meet on one side. Sad to part on the other.

Here's a story about that.

Friends moving away

Sam was standing in a corner of the playground with tears in his eyes, when Mr Gordon the caretaker spotted him. Mr Gordon was good at spotting children who were upset. Sometimes he chatted to them himself, sometimes he spoke to the headteacher about them. He knew Sam quite well, so he decided to have a word with him.

'What's up, Sam? Don't tell me, I can guess. I reckon you're missing Wesley.'

Sam nodded. Wesley was his best friend. They had been inseparable all the way through infants school and then for two years of junior school. They went everywhere together – in class, in the playground, in school plays, everything.

Then Wesley's family decided to move back to St Lucia. 'It's warmer there,' said Wesley's mum. 'And it's a bit slower and a bit less dangerous than it is here in the city. So we're going back. Anyway, Dad wants to go home, so we're going.'

Wesley wasn't at all sure about this. He'd been to St Lucia on holiday and he'd had great fun, and got on with all his family there. But going there for good? Wesley was a bit upset himself.

Sam and his family had gone to see Wesley and his family off at Gatwick Airport. They had enjoyed an hour or two there, before they had to go up on the open deck, looking at the planes and laughing just as they always had. Then Sam had queued with the family at the check-in desk, surrounded by people with lots of luggage, going off to the Caribbean. And that had been a laugh too.

But then there had come the awful moment, that kept coming back to Sam – when Wesley

and his family had gone through the doors into the departure lounge. A quick look back, and a wave and he was gone. Just like that. Gone. 'And I won't see him again, ever,' said Sam a little tearfully to Mr Gordon.

'Well,' said Mr Gordon. 'That's never certain is it. All kinds of things can happen. Still, it doesn't do to keep wishing someone would come back when they've gone. You have to accept that they've gone, and that they're not coming back, and you have to decide what the best way is that you can cope with that.'

'That doesn't help,' said Sam.

'Of course not,' said Mr Gordon. 'It takes time. Nobody says you can't be upset. Nobody says you can't cry or talk about Wesley. Just accepting that he's gone is difficult enough. Now, let me tell you about what happens to you as you go through life. Let me tell you about some of my friends.'

Sam nodded.

'A long, long time ago now, I was in the army. I did my National Service – we all had to do two years in the forces then. I went to Catterick in Yorkshire and did my basic training. I made friends with three other lads – David, Bas and Trevor. We became really close. Then we were posted to Malaya together, and we stayed there for nearly two years. We were always together – I've got lots of photographs. They were terrific friends to me – loyal and good fun. We worked together and we went out together in the evenings.

'Then our time there ended and we flew back together to the transit camp in Chester. On our last day in the Army we said goodbye, and went our separate ways – we all came from

Friends moving away

completely different parts of the country – and we've never seen each other from that day to this. We each had different lives to lead. Dave went to Oxford and ended up in the BBC. Bas became a teacher and Trevor went to work in his dad's garage in Scotland. We sent cards occasionally, and once we talked on the phone about the possibility of meeting, but it never happened. We each built our own life, with new friends, and families.'

Sam looked at Mr Gordon. 'So it's as if you'd never met really?'

'Oh dear, no,' said Mr Gordon. 'They were great times we had, and their faces are very clear in my mind, even now. In a way they are still there with me, just as they were then. The funny thing is I remember them as they were then – when we were nineteen years old. Now we're all fifty something, and they'll be very different. But I cherish the memory of them as they were. It's part of the whole stock of memories that I've built up through life. We were good friends for a while, and in my memory we'll be good friends for ever.'

'Will Wesley be like that?' asked Sam.

'I guess so. He'll always be the same in your mind as he was when you were here together. Even when you're grown up. And gradually you'll both make new friends and go on your own journey through life. But it's so good that you knew each other. You learned a lot from each other, and that won't go away.'

When a good friend of yours, or even your best friend, moves away you're bound to feel sad and all of us in school know that. We'll try and help and we'll make sure you have other friends who will be there to talk and play with you. You'll miss your old friend but remember

the story and think how your friend will always be in your memories – and you'll probably see each other again, anyway!

☀ A prayer

Dear God, we thank you for friendship and love and loyalty. We thank you for laughter and good memories. Be with our friends when they leave us to go on their own journeys, and keep good memories alive in their hearts and in ours. Amen.

☀ A thought

It's good to make friends and sometimes we make very special friends. But there may be times when we have to say goodbye to our special friends. Let's remember the good times we spent together and know that we will always have those memories. What matters is that we can deal with our partings, and accept them and go on to new things.

© **pfp** 2002 ISBN 1 874050 57 0 May be photocopied for use only within the purchasing institution **pfp**, 61 Gray's Inn Road, London WC1X 8TH

Young carers

© pfp 2002 ISBN 1 874050 57 0

✦ Introduction

This is an assembly about young carers – young people whose lives are restricted because they have considerable responsibility for someone in the family who needs special care.

Aims:

The aims of this assembly are to

- raise awareness among staff and pupils of the difficulties of young carers

- let pupils who are, or who may become, carers know that others are in the same situation, and that there are people who can help.

✦ Background

No one is really sure how many young carers there are, although estimates run between 15,000 and 40,000. The majority of them will be in secondary schools, but some will be in primary classrooms. Young carers often find that the family doctor and perhaps their social worker are too busy to give them the support they need.

At one level, a child may find that a happy, carefree time with an indulgent father has vanished overnight, because of the father's illness. At another, a girl may have been struggling alone for some time with the personal needs of a mother who has MS.

In some ways, they represent a forgotten section of the community – they tend not to talk much about what they do, except perhaps sometimes to close friends, and even then, because it is difficult for other children to understand what happens, the whole story does not really come out. There are other reasons for silence – fear that the family may be split up, for example, or simple pride. It can also be particularly difficult to identify young carers in ethnic minority communities.

The sense of loneliness and isolation which can be felt by young carers is often unrecognised in schools and this assembly helps bring the issue into the open, without putting the spotlight on any particular child.

(There is a list of further resources and organisations in Appendix 3, Young carers on page 159.)

✦ Before the assembly

Talk to staff about the existence of young carers in school. Be prepared to modify the assembly appropriately if you or your staff have knowledge of known carers in your school.

Optional If you have a very good reader in Year 5 or 6, you may like to ask them beforehand to read the quote from the carer.

Young carers

📖 **The assembly**

We talk a lot in school about caring. We think of ourselves as a caring community – by which we mean that we are interested in each other and like to help each other whenever we can. If one of us has a problem, then others will come forward to help – at least we hope that's what will happen, because that is what being part of a caring community means.

For most of your lives as children you have been cared for, haven't you? When you were a tiny baby you could do very little for yourself – you had to be bathed and fed and have your nappy changed. Now you're a bit bigger you don't need some of these things done for you. But I bet you still feel the need to be looked after – someone to get your food, sort your clothes out, see you off in the morning, solve your problems.

Let me ask you this, though. Could you do it for someone else? Could you really look after someone else? Of course you could, if you had to. You could look after your mum or your dad or your gran, or your brother or sister if they needed looking after for a bit. Perhaps you already do it – perhaps you help your gran, or your young brother or sister. Perhaps you help your mum or your dad when there are things that you can do and they can't.

Mind you, it would affect your life a bit wouldn't it? We'll look at exactly how, a little later.

Sometimes, for some young people, caring for someone else in the family becomes a permanent and quite difficult job. It starts to get in the way of other parts of the young person's life – school work, going out with friends, taking part in sport. Let me tell you about a couple of young carers.

Jessica is thirteen and she helps to look after her young sister, Becky, who is ten, but who needs lots of extra help. Becky acts a lot younger than she is and she can't walk very well. Jessica helps Becky to dress, brush her teeth and go to the toilet. Jessica has to be really patient, because Becky can be very moody and sometimes has tantrums. It can be very difficult at times, because Jessica finds that Becky's needs have to come first in the family, and so there are many occasions when she can't do the things that she wants to do. But the family all love Becky, and so they go on doing their best for her.

• • • • • • • • • • • •

Georgie is eight and his dad has had a severe stroke, which means that he can't talk or move very well. Life is not the same for Georgie any more, because instead of his dad being able to take him out and do all the good things they used to do together, he now has to stay at home and be looked after, and Georgie joins in the caring. Things have changed so much.

Young carers like Jessica and Georgie don't talk about their lives very much. There are lots of reasons for this. One of them is that people just don't understand. It's really difficult for other people to understand what it's like for a young person to have to care for an adult.

This is how one young carer explained it.

• • • • • • • • • • • •

Optional *(Name)* is going to read her words to you.

Can you picture an adult who is unable to stand or walk by herself?

Young carers

Can you picture what might happen at bedtime?

Can you picture the adult's young daughter picking up her mum and carrying her to the bottom of the stairs and putting her on the stairlift?

Can you picture the young daughter picking her mum off the stairlift at the top of the stairs and carrying her into the bathroom?

Can you picture the young daughter helping her mum to go to the toilet, and then helping her into the bath and bathing her, just as her mum bathed her when she was a baby and her mum was well?

Can you picture all of this?

Perhaps you can't.

Perhaps it is all too far from the life that you know and understand.

But if you find it difficult to picture all of that, then perhaps you can understand why we don't talk about it much, because nobody really knows what it is like.

Pause.

Now think about that young daughter's life.

How easy is it for her to do her homework?

Can she have a Saturday job or an evening job?

Can she have a boyfriend?

Will she always be on time for school, every day?

Can she be in the school play?

Will her mum take her shopping for new shoes at Christmas?

Sometimes, there are extra problems. There may not be enough money in the house, because disabled people sometimes cannot work and may have to live on social security.

Does anyone help?

Well, of course, there are the social services, and disabled people do get help – the stairlift that this lady uses was put in because social services knew that she had to have one. The bathroom and toilet were made easier to use. People from the social services call in and help, especially during the day.

But sometimes, the young carer would like somebody to talk to her about her own life and her own problems. Sometimes she feels a bit lonely and a bit forgotten.

The good news is that there are people who can help. There is the Young Carers National Association, for example, which puts young carers in touch with people who understand, and makes sure that they are getting all the help and support that they need.

If anyone here knows anyone who would like to know about Young Carers National Association, then see me and I will not only give you the address, but help with any letters that need writing or phone calls that have to be made.

Of course, not all young carers feel forgotten and lonely. Some find that caring for someone in their family can have a positive effect, and that they've grown up as a result of this extra responsibility. They have become more tolerant and patient of other people, and have

Young carers

developed skills that they did not know they had.

But still, if you know anyone who is in this situation, who is a young carer, the nice thing is that you can care for them too. When you can, make sure that you are kind to them and support them, and make sure they have fun and someone to talk to, who will try to understand.

Now let's have a **prayer/special thought** about young carers.

☀ A prayer

Dear God, we think our school is a caring community. But sometimes it's as if we do not really know what real caring is. Looking after a little sister who cannot walk properly, or a dad who has had a stroke, or a mum who cannot move easily – that's what real caring is. Help us think about young people all over the world whose own lives are restricted by the loving care that they give to others. Let them know that your love and understanding are with them and help us to make them feel that they are not alone. Amen.

☀ A thought

We think our school is a caring community. But sometimes it's as if we do not really know what real caring is. Looking after a little sister who cannot walk properly, or a dad who has had a stroke, or a mum who cannot move easily – that's what real caring is. Let's think about young people all over the world whose own lives are restricted by the loving care that they give to others. Let's make sure that if we can, we help them feel that they are not alone and that someone understands them and can help.

Appendix 1

✦ Children and divorce

Divorce (we use the word here to include separation) can be a long drawn out and unhappy business, and there can be no doubt that it affects children.

Younger children, particularly, just do not understand what is happening to their parents, and this makes them feel confused, angry and afraid. They often also feel guilty – in the absence of any other explanation that makes sense in childhood terms, the children begin to think that they must have done something to cause the break up.

Even when the children are treated with the utmost consideration, the children of divorced parents are inevitably going to face a difficult set of adjustments at every level, emotional and practical. It can take up to two or three years for a child to come to terms with all of this.

For all children, and especially for younger ones, divorce can cause feelings that are akin to the feelings of bereavement – bewilderment, and guilt – 'was it something I did or did not do?' As with bereavement, therefore, an important priority in dealing with the children of a divorce is to provide accurate information supported by reassurance. Honesty builds trust, and is the best way to head off feelings of guilt and fear.

Unlike bereavement, though, divorce has another dimension. It may represent the ending of a period of domestic strife and argument – even violence – which is in itself damaging to children. Constant disputes between parents can cause children to feel helpless. 'I don't like this. I just want it to stop, and yet I can do nothing about it.'

This helplessness easily leads to a lowering of self-esteem – and children may start to seek attention by being unnaturally good or bad. They may become extremely quiet, withdrawn and isolated. In any of these circumstances their school work is going to be affected.

When this is so, the final separation, difficult though it may be to cope with, provides an opportunity for both children and adults to rebuild on different foundations.

What can teachers do, assuming that they know what is happening at home?

The priority, as for all children under stress, is to provide stability, understanding and a listening ear. Established routines are important, as is the presence of familiar teachers and other staff. It follows that all staff with significant dealings with a child troubled in this way, should know what is going on, and understand the possible consequences for behaviour. The aim is to provide a balance between care, affection and understanding and expectations about work and behaviour.

It is important that teachers should feel able to talk with children who are troubled about breakdown at home. Children need to know that someone is listening and want to hear that their distress is normal, and that they should not feel guilty about it. This is not just a matter of a quiet word at playtime. Classwork comes into the picture too, and teachers should consider offering activities that

- enable children experiencing the process of a divorce or marital strife, to express their feelings

- allow for the building of stronger self-confidence and self-esteem

© pfp 2002 ISBN 1 874050 57 0 May be photocopied for use only within the purchasing institution **pfp**, 61 Gray's Inn Road, London WC1X 8TH
Appendix 1   **145**

Appendix 2

- help children to sort out their beliefs and attitudes towards separation and divorce

- provide positive distractions from the over-riding problems that they are facing at home.

The school must also keep open lines of communication with the child's parents. Sometimes this is not easy, especially if there is anger and the adults are blaming each other for the negative response of their child.

Communication is important, in particular, because the school needs to have early warning of difficulties and events that might affect the child's welfare and behaviour.

It is worth remembering that around one in eight children in primary schools is likely to have experienced divorce and that evidence suggests that it is an extremely stressful time for them. Even when parents are unhappy and aggressive towards each other, children want their parents to stay together. The key thing is that it is almost inevitable that divorce will cause problems for the child in school and that their behaviour will change.

It is often the stability and caring approach of the teacher which help the child come through this very difficult time successfully.
(For suggested resources on this subject, see pages 148–149.)

Appendix 2

✦ Children and bereavement

Most of us find the link between children and death very difficult to make, so we tend to keep our thoughts on the two well separated. As a result it can escape our attention that children face bereavement – and separations which are akin to bereavement – more often than most adults realise. Divorce, long distance house moves, hospitalisations and death (including the death of beloved pets) all bring about feelings of loss with which children find it difficult to cope.

The first thing to realise is that bereaved children may not behave as adults do. Adults, in a sense, have the vocabulary for grief – they have seen it in others, and experienced it second hand in fiction and drama. They know what it is, and they have an idea of the range of behaviours that are available.

Children do not have this understanding. A grieving child does not really know what the feeling is – has no name for it, and no knowledge of whether it is acceptable or right. For all the child knows, crying and being upset may be bad, or frowned upon. As a result, the child may bottle feelings up. And if adults are trying not to show their feelings, or avoid any talk about the loss 'for children's sake', then those children may feel that their own grieving is somehow wrong and unacceptable, and they will bottle it up even more.

This bottled up emotion may well, of course, emerge in other ways. A grieving child may misbehave, or regress to an earlier stage of development.

Teachers should therefore address these points.

1 Recognise that children react to bereavement in different ways – withdrawal, anger, panic, fear, inattention.

Age is a factor – young children find it difficult to see death as permanent.

Older infants and younger juniors gradually become aware of the finality of death, and can be very curious about the details. At this age, too, they are quite likely to be distressed by perceived links between what they did or thought and the person's death – 'I was angry because she told me off, and she died.' Adults sometimes do this, but children are more likely to.

Older juniors and secondary pupils begin to see death as adults do.

2 Tackle the issue – to ignore grief in a child is to give the message that the event is not important. As the experts say, it is impossible not to communicate, and so to say nothing is to belittle the child's feelings. But also remember that when a child has lost a parent or another significant adult, it is important to establish continuity in the child's daily routine.

3 Reassure children of your being able to care for their needs, and the fact that they will not be abandoned. Both at school and at home, children need to know that they will be well looked after and cared for, and that they will have as much stability as is possible in their lives during this difficult time.

4 If the rest of the class or the school has to be told that a child is grieving, then consult the child first as to how this might be done. The usual way is to tell the group separately while the child is out of the room.

5 Do not be too ready to believe that a child is recovering well. Adults can indulge in wishful thinking – they want the child to be OK, and so they say that 'he's coping wonderfully'. In fact, the child might be bottling up his or her feelings to protect the feelings of adults, and may in fact be sleeping badly and lacking

concentration. It may take a child months even to accept what has happened. The word 'numb' comes up frequently in their own descriptions.

6 Give honest answers. Grieving children deserve them. Use the word 'death' for example. Phrases such as 'lost', 'sleeping', 'gone away' can deceive a child, especially a young one, into thinking that the dead person is coming back, or has decided to go off somewhere without the child. This can increase feelings of guilt – 'Why did mummy go without me, or without telling me?'

7 Let the children know how death happens. They need to understand that death results from real, physical causes, and not because of anything that they have said or done. Children also need to know about funerals and burial, so that they are not disturbed by these rites.

8 Include death in the curriculum. Experts in this field believe that schools should teach about death, just as they teach about sex, birth and marriage. They point out how illogical it is that one certain thing about humanity – that we will all eventually die – figures nowhere in the school curriculum. Even the youngest child can be told about death, using opportunities in nature – the death of a class pet, or of a bird; the life cycle of a flower. There can be class discussion about such things.

In summary, there are four main stages of bereavement.

SHOCK when there is denial by the child, and they sometimes seem to carry on as if nothing has happened. This can last for a few hours or a few weeks.

ANGER AND UNFAIRNESS when there is the sense of injustice and sometimes the need to blame somebody else. Children may actually feel ill during this stage.

Appendix 3

SADNESS, SORROW AND LONGING
which is usually a longer stage and
characterised by feelings of depression
and aloneness.

REBUILDING which usually occurs by the
end of the first year, and sees children
beginning to be more optimistic and recovering
from their grief.

These stages are set out more fully in Childhood
Stress by Pippa Alsop and Trisha McCaffrey
(1993) Longman.
In this difficult and stressful time it is the role of
the teacher to help the bereaved child through
his or her pain rather than trying to avoid it or
remove it.
*(For suggested resources on this subject,
see pages 150–151.)*

Appendix 3

✦ Divorce

Children often suffer from the effects of
divorce as it causes distress and confusion.
Below are some addresses and publications to
prepare what children need when their parents
or carers are splitting up.

Organisations

CHILDLINE
Tel: 0800 1111 www.childline.org.uk
- free 24-hour national helpline
- children or young people can talk to
  someone about something they are
  worried or frightened about.

CHILDREN'S LEGAL CENTRE
Tel: 01206 873820
www.childrenslegalcentre.com
- free advice and information on laws
  affecting children and young people

Address – administration
Childline HQ, Studd Street, London,
N1 0QW. Tel: 020 7239 1000.

Address – for children
Childline, Freepost 1111, London N1 0BR.

CITIZENS ADVICE BUREAU
CHILD AND FAMILY GUIDANCE
COURT WELFARE SERVICE
SOCIAL SERVICES
also offer help and advice. The numbers
will be found in the local phone directory.

**THE CHILDREN'S SOCIETY AND
PEOPLE PROJECTS**
have produced a pack designed to help families
with the stress of separation and divorce.

**Focus on families: divorce and its
effects on children**
A briefing paper by Erica De'Ath suggests
ways forward, and sets out historical and
sociological explanations about the research
that has been conducted. Available from

**Publications Department, The Children's
Society, Edward Rudolf House, Margery
Street, London WC1X 0JL.
Tel: 020 7841 4436
www.the-childrens-society.org.uk
Email: info@childrenssociety.org.uk**

Publications

For children and young people

All available from the Relate Bookshop, Herbert Gray College, Little Church Street, Rugby CV21 3AP. Tel: 01788 563816 www.relate.org.uk

Children Don't Divorce by R Stones (1991) Happy Cat Books

Since Dad Left by C Birich (1995) Frances Lincoln

How do I feel about my parents' divorce by J Cole (1994) Watts

What About Me? by J Collinson (1991)
Available from Northumberland & Tyneside Family Mediation Service, 4th Floor, MEA House, Ellinson Place, Newcastle upon Tyne. Tel: 0191 261 9212.

Mike's Lonely Summer – A Child's Guide through Divorce by C Nystrom (1994)
Available from Lion Publishing, Mayfield House, 256 Banbury Road, Oxford, OX2 5DH. Tel: 01865 302750. www.lion-publishing.co.uk

It's My Life by R Leeson (1983)
Available from Harper Collins Publishers Ltd, Westerhill Road, Glasgow G64 2QT. Tel: 0870 0100 442. www.fireandwater.com

It's Not The End of the World by J Blume (1998)
Available from MacMillan's Children's Books, c/o MacMillan Distribution Ltd, Brunel Road, Basingstoke, Hants RG21 6XS. Tel: 01256 302692. www.macmillan.co.uk

Buddy by N Hinton (1996)
Available from Puffin Books, 27 Wright's Lane, London W8 5TZ.

Holding Me Here by P Conrad (1990)
Available from Puffin Books, 80 Strand, London WC2R 0RL. Tel: 020 7010 3000. www.puffin.co.uk

Parents Are Forever by P Thomas (1995) and The Divorce Book by McKay et al (1985)
Both available from the Relate Bookshop, Herbert Gray College, Little Church Street, Rugby CV21 3AP. Tel: 01788 563816. www.relate.org.uk

For parents and carers

Helping Children Cope With Divorce by R Wells (1997)
Available from Sheldon Press, Holy Trinity Church, Marylebone Rd, London NW1 4DU. Tel: 020 7387 5282. www.spckonline.com

Me in My Changing Family by B Bathey (1989)
Available from Family Mediation Scotland, 18 York Place, Edinburgh EH1 3EP. Tel: 0131 558 9898. www.familymediationscotland.org.uk

The following books are all available from the Relate Bookshop, details above.

Children, Feelings and Divorce by Heather Smith (1999) Free Association Books

What to tell the kids about your divorce by Darlene Weyburne (1993) New Harbinger Publications

Don't divorce your children by J Lewis & W Sammons (2000) Contemporary Books

But I Want to Stay With You... talking with children about separation and divorce, by Jill Burrett (2000) Simon and Schuster

Appendix 3

✦ Bereavement

Many children find it very difficult to cope with grief. Depending on their age, children deal with grief in many ways, often through not accepting that someone they cared for has actually gone.

The addresses and publications listed on this page may give
- advice to help children, teachers, parents or carers
- support and counselling
- other organisations than those listed as they are all aware of each other

Local Authority Educational Psychologists may or may not be equipped to advise schools on bereavement.

A local hospice, the Acorn Children's Hospice in the Midlands, for example, can be a good starting point.

- Acorn produces a superb pack for schools with a large collection of pamphlets and reprints on family grief and bereavement.
- Acorn also provides courses for professionals – details on request.

Available from Jayne Adams (Education Liaison Officer) at Acorn, 103 Oak Tree Lane, Selly Oak, Birmingham B29 6HZ.

Organisations

WINSTON'S WISH

Gloucestershire Royal Hospital, Great Western Road, Gloucester GL1 3NN.
Tel: 01452 394165.
www.winstonswish.org.uk

This organisation organises residential camps for bereaved children, and supports schools in its area. They produce a pack which includes a very practical 'strategy for schools'.

THE COMPASSIONATE FRIENDS

53 North Street, Bristol BS3 1EN.
Tel: 0117 966 5202 (office)
0117 953 9639 (helpline).
www.tcf.org.uk   email: info@tcf.org.uk

An international organisation of bereaved parents (some local groups).
Excellent short publications.

CRUSE – Bereavement Care

Cruse House, 126 Sheen Road, Richmond, Surrey TW9 1UR. Tel: 020 8940 4818.
Bereavement helpline: 020 8332 7227.
www.crusebereavementcare.org.uk
email: info@crusebereavementcare.org.uk

This is an organisation that offers help to anyone who is unfortunate enough to lose a loved one and there are branches throughout the UK.

Publications

Each of these gives further reading lists and addresses of organisations.

Death and Loss – Compassionate Approaches in the Classroom by Oliver Leaman (1995)
Available from Continuum c/o Orca Book Services, Stanley House, 3 Fleets Lane, Poole BH15 3AJ. Tel: 01202 665432.

The Forgotten Mourners by Sister Margaret Pennells and Susan C Smith (1995)
Available from CRUSE and Jessica Kingsley Publishers, 116 Pentonville Road, London N1 9JB. Tel: 020 7833 2307.

'Good Grief 1'(1995) and 'Good Grief 2' by Barbara Ward and Associates (1996)
For working with under–elevens and over–elevens, a very popular teacher's pack. Available from CRUSE and Jessica Kingsley Publishers, 116 Pentonville Road, London N1 9JB. Tel: 020 7833 2307.

Appendix 3

For children and schools:

All the following publications are available from CRUSE. Here is a list of recommended books on loss and bereavement for children and teenagers, along with descriptions.

Supporting Bereaved Children and Families: A Training Manual from CRUSE Consultant Editor: Dr Dora Black (1993)

- essential knowledge base on which counselling skills with children and their families can be built

The Drawing Out Feelings Series by Marge Heegaard (1992)

- offers an organised approach to helping 6–12 year olds with mixed feelings resulting from family loss and change
- a series of workbooks
1 When someone very special dies
2 When someone has a very serious illness
3 When something terrible happens

The Facilitator Guide for Drawing Out Feelings (1992)

- guide for professionals who are using the workbooks above
- includes ideas for six structured sessions with grieving children

Caring for bereaved children by Mary Bending (1998)

- concise booklet by a CRUSE counsellor which enables parents, relatives, teachers and carers to understand the child's grief
- suggests ways of helping
- covers age groups from birth up to and including adolescence

If You Have Children – Some Practical Advice to Widowers by Susan Wallbank

For under 7 years of age

Badger's Parting Gifts by S Varley (1984) Picture Lions

- colourful and beautiful illustrations
- realistic and hopeful

Grandpa by J Burningham (1989) Puffin

- simple words
- delightful illustrations

Remembering Mum by Ginny Perkins & Leon Morris (1991) A & C Black

- for children aged approximately 3–10 years of age
- coloured photos and simple text describe an ordinary day in their lives and many ways in which they remember their mum

Remembering my brother by Ginny Perkins and Leon Morris (1996) A & C Black

- a family remembering a loss in positive ways

Waterbugs and Dragonflies by D Stickney (1984) Pilgrim Press/United Church Press

- short and simple, a book that helps explain death to young children
- black and white illustrations which can be coloured in by child
- Christian interpretation and a prayer if required

For 7–11 year olds

Charlotte's Web by EB White (1993) Puffin

- a rich, fairly complex story

What do we think about... Death by Karen Bryant-Mole (2000) Hodder Wayland

- multi-ethnic
- coloured photos
- suitable for 8–14 year olds

Appendix 3

✦ Drugs

Below are examples of the help that is available. The type of help can vary from agency to agency, but many offer more than one service. These include

- general advice and information
- support and counselling

Services are provided from a number of different locations. The services are not only for the person with the problem, but also for parents, carers, friends and relatives.

Organisations

Locally

Some LEAs have health or drug education advisors to provide training, advice and information about drug education. Every area now has a Drug Action Team to coordinate action about drugs. Your local Health Promotion Unit will be able to provide information, leaflets, posters and other educational materials. They will be in the phone book under your local health authority. The youth and community section of the local police may send a police officer to help run a lesson about the legal aspect of drugs.

Nationally

THE NATIONAL DRUGS HELPLINE

Tel: 0800 77 66 00 www.ndh.org.uk

- free advice about drugs
- any information you need to know about drugs
- lines are open 24 hours a day, every day and anyone may call
- all calls are free and confidential
- printed literature free of charge
- confidential counselling available

THE STANDING CONFERENCE ON DRUG ABUSE (SCODA)

Waterbridge House, 32–36 Loman Street, London SE1 0EE. Tel: 020 7928 9500. www.ncvovol.org.uk/main/gateway/subsites/scoda.html
email: info@scoda.demon.co.uk

- an independent national coordinating body for drug services
- specialist advice on local services
- best practice information on drug treatment and care, prevention and education

DRUGSCOPE

Waterbridge House, 32–36 Loman Street, London SE1 0EE. Tel: 020 7928 1211. www.drugscope.org.uk
email: services@drugscope.org.uk

- comprehensive library service
- research department for information on the use and misuse of drugs.

There are also support services for families of drug users such as

ADFAM NATIONAL

Waterbridge House, 32–36 Loman Street, London SE1 0EE. Tel: 0207 928 8900. www.rexsoft.com/adfam.htm

- charity for the families and friends of drug users
- offers confidential support and information
- callers can ring as often as they need
- ADFAM will call back if the cost of the call is ever a problem

FAMILIES ANONYMOUS

Tel: 020 7498 4680

- self-help support group for parents of drug users
- branches in various parts of the country

Publications available from ADFAM

The ADFAM Family Support Group Pack

- a guide to help set up/run a family support group

Living with a drug user

- a booklet for partners of drug users

Booklet for the parents and carers of drug users are also available.

RELEASE

Tel: 0808 8000 800
Drugs in School Helpline hours: 10:00 am to 5:00 pm, Monday to Friday
www.release.org.uk

- 24-hour confidential helpline (020 7729 9904)
- provides advice on drug use for those concerned with a drug incident in school

For services in Scotland:

THE SCOTTISH DRUGS FORUM

5th Floor, Shaftesbury House, 5 Waterloo Street, Glasgow G2 6AY. Tel: 0141 221 1175.
www.sdf.org.uk

For services in Wales

THE NATIONAL ASSEMBLY FOR WALES

Cardiff Bay, Cardiff CF99 1NA
Tel: 029 20 825111. www.wales.gov.uk

For services in Northern Ireland

HEALTH PROMOTION BRANCH

DHSS, Upper Newtownards Road, Belfast BT4 3SF. Tel: 028 9052 4234.

Teaching packs

The Good Health Guide to Drugs by T Brown and J Bennett (1995) (video and teachers' guide)

Available from the Educational Television Company, PO Box 100, Warwick CV34 6TZ.
Tel: 01926 433333.

The Primary School Drugs Pack by J Cohen, S Scott and J Kay (1995)

Available from Healthwise Ltd, 9 Slater Street, Liverpool L1 4BW. Tel: 0151 703 7700.
www.healthwise.org.uk

Skills for the Primary School Child 3: The World of Drugs by A Moon (1996)

Available from Tacade, 1 Hulme Place, The Crescent, Salford M5 4QA.
Tel: 0161 745 8925. www.tacade.com

Drugs Education: A Practical Guide for Primary School Teachers by T Taylor (1996)

Available from Groups in Learning, 10 Charlotte Street, Bristol BS1 5PX.
Tel: 0117 941 5859.

For parents, teachers and other adults

The Health Education Authority (1996) A parents' guide to drugs and solvents.

Available free on the National Drugs Helpline.

DFES materials

Drug Prevention and Schools (1995) Circular ref CIR004/95
Drug Education – Getting the message across ref GTMADRUG
Drug Education: Curriculum Guidance for Schools (1995) Ref: PPY087
Digest of Drug Education Resources (1995) Ref: PPY088
Innovation in Drug Education ref PPY376
Drug Education in Schools Ref: PPY385
Protecting Young People – Good Practice in Drug Education Ref: PPPDRUGS
The Right Choice – Guidance on Drug Education Materials Ref: TRCDRUG

**All available free from the Department for Education and Skills Publication Order Line, PO Box 5050, Sherwood Business Park, Annesley, Nottingham NG15 0DJ.
Tel: 0845 602 2260. www.dfes.gov.uk
Public Enquiry Unit: 0870 000 2288.**

Appendix 3

✦ Mental health

Organisations

MIND
Granta House, 15–19 Broadway, Stratford,
London E15 4BQ. Tel: 020 8519 2122.
Helpline: 020 8522 1728.
www.mind.org.uk

MANIC DEPRESSION FELLOWSHIP
Castle Works, 21 St George's Road,
London SE1 6ES. Tel: 020 7793 2600.
www.mdf.org.uk email: mdf@mdf.org.uk

MDF is an organisation that
• provides support, advice and an
  information leaflet for young people with
  a parent with manic depression

YOUNGMINDS (Children's Mental Health Charity)

102–108 Clerkenwell Road, London
EC1M 5SA. Tel: 020 7336 8445.
Helpline: 0800 018 2138.
www.youngminds.org.uk

NATIONAL SCHIZOPHRENIA FELLOWSHIP

28 Castle Street, Kingston upon Thames,
Surrey KT1 1SS. Tel: 020 8547 3937.
www.nsf.org.uk email: info@nsf.org.uk
An association that gives help and advice to
people affected by mental illness.

SANE

1st Floor, Cityside House, 40 Adler Street,
London E1 1EE. Tel: 020 7375 1002.
www.sane.org.uk
Saneline: 0845 767 8000
This organisation offers
• a confidential helpline giving local help
• talk with someone who understands about
  mental illness
• help for young people who need someone
  to talk to

Publications

Contact YoungMinds for a range of
publications including

Booklets for children, for example
• mental illness in your family
• do you ever feel depressed?
• in school, stay cool

Information leaflets for adults, for example
• Why do young minds matter?
• Children and young people get
  depressed too
and a magazine, resources sheets and books.

✦ Abuse/Violence

Organisations

CHILD LINE
Studd Street, London N1 0QW.
Administration Dept: 020 7239 1000
Address for children
Freepost 1111, London N1 0BR.
Helpline: 0800 1111 (24-hour)

The following publications are available from
The Children's Society, Edward Rudolf House,
Margery Street, London WC1X 0JL.
Tel: 020 7841 4400.

Suitable for children aged 4–9 years

Mousie by Khadi Rouf (1989)
• fully illustrated storybook
• encourages children to speak out
• a valuable resource

My Book My Body by Anne Peake (1989)
• highly popular colouring book
• helps children to talk about feelings

Suitable for children aged 8–16 years

Secrets by Khadi Rouf (1989)
• picture-strip style
• ethnic mix

Our Girls' Group written by a group of girls, edited by Anne Peake (1989)

Holding His Mask written by boys and girls, edited by Anne Peake (1989)

- encourages young people to talk about their experiences.

Your local library may have related resources.

✦ Bullying

Publications

Bullying: a Practical Guide to Coping for Schools edited by Michele Elliott (1996) Financial Times Prentice Hall

- latest thinking and research from educationalists and child care professionals
- ways in which bullies can be helped
- strategies schools can develop to approach the problem of bullying in schools

Available from Pearson Education, Edinburgh Gate, Harlow, Essex CM20 2JE. Tel: 0800 579579.

Lucky Duck Publishing provide a wide range of resources, including INSET materials on bullying and related areas such as self-esteem, behaviour management and emotional literacy. They can be contacted at Lucky Duck Publishing, 3 Thorndale Mews, Clifton, Bristol BS8 2HX. Tel: 0117 973 2881. www.luckyduck.co.uk

Examples of publications include

- Safe to Tell (2000) – Producing an effective anti-bullying policy in schools by Barbara Maines and George Robinson (2000)
- The Bullying Booklist, compiled by Jane Doggett and published for the Gloucestershire School Library Service, is a collection of resources and books for children and adults and includes stories, information books, videos, as well as useful organisations.

Jenny Mosley Consultancies are well known for a range of high-quality resources regarding self-esteem, Circle Time and related issues such as bullying. They can be contacted at

Positive Press Ltd/Jenny Mosley Consultancies
28a Gloucester Road, Trowbridge, Wiltshire BA14 0AA
Tel: 01225 719204 for resources.
Tel: 01225 767157 for INSET.

Visit www.booktrusted.com for a comprehensive listing of books concerning bullying, segregated into picture books/junior fiction/senior fiction and non-fiction.

✦ AIDS/HIV

Organisations

THE TERRENCE HIGGINS TRUST
52–54 Gray's Inn Road, London WC1X 8JU.
Information Line: 020 7831 0330
(10:00 am to 5:00 pm on weekdays).
Helpline: 020 7242 1010
(12 noon to 10:00 pm 7 days a week).
www.tht.org.uk email: info@tht.org.uk

- one of the largest charities for people affected by HIV infection and AIDS in London
- strictly confidential telephone service
- up-to-date information and advice

NATIONAL AIDS HELPLINE
1st Cavencourt, 8 Matthew Street, Liverpool L2 6RE.
Freephone: 0800 567123 (24 hrs).

WAVERLEY CARE TRUST
4a Royal Terrace, Edinburgh EH7 5AB.
Tel: 0131 556 3959.

Appendix 3

Publications

The following are available from The Terrence Higgins Trust.

Understanding HIV Infection and AIDS (1995)
- general information about HIV and AIDS

Aids in the family (1994)
- information for parents and carers of children

Children Act briefing: A guide for workers in the field (1993)
- summarises the main provisions of the Children Act and gives examples of the ways in which it affects children and families with HIV or AIDS

What can I do about Aids? (1995)
- booklet produced with Barnardo's for 11–14 year olds, answering questions about AIDS

There is also The Terrence Higgins Trust Library Service which has details of more resources that may be available. A leaflet with details of counselling services is also available.

✦ Special needs

Some children and adults find learning things and coping with ordinary life more difficult than others.

People with special needs all require some sort of help. The extent of that help depends largely on how disabled the person actually is.

These organisations below offer help and guidance for parents, children and carers, regardless of who actually has a disability.

Organisations

ADD INFORMATION SERVICES
PO Box 340, Edgware, Middlesex HA8 9HL.
Tel: 020 8906 9068. Fax: 020 8959 0727.
email: info@addiss.co.uk. www.addiss.co.uk
Information and support related to attention deficit disorder.

AFASIC
50–52 Great Sutton Street, London
EC1U 0DJ. Tel: 020 7490 9410.
Fax: 020 7251 2834.
email: info@afasic.org.uk www.afasic.org.uk
Association for all speech impaired children.
Information and advice.

ASBAH
42 Park Road, Peterborough, Cambridgeshire
PE1 2YQ. Tel: 01733 555988.
Fax: 01733 555985.
email: postmaster@asbah.org www.asbah.org
Association for spina bifida and hydrocephalus.
Information, support and publications.

CHILD LINE
Studd Street, London N1 0QW.
Tel: 020 7239 1000. Fax: 020 7239 1001.
www.childline.org.uk
Helpline for children needing support.

CONTACT A FAMILY
209–211 City Road, London WC1V 1JN.
Tel: 020 7608 8700. Fax: 020 7608 8701.
email: info@cafamily.org.uk.
www.cafamily.org.uk
Support for families of children with special needs.

COUNCIL FOR DISABLED CHILDREN
National Children's Bureau, 8 Wakley Street,
London EC1V 7QE. Tel: 020 7843 6000.
Fax: 020 7278 9512.
email: membership@ncb.org.uk.
www.ncb.org.uk
Information about services and facilities.

Appendix 3

CROSSROADS CARE

10 Regent Place, Rugby, Warwickshire
CV21 2PN. Tel: 01788 573653.
www.crossroads.org.uk
Support for carers of all ages, who are looking
after someone with a disability – Crossroads
Care will help to relieve the carers.

DOWN'S SYNDROME ASSOCIATION

155 Mitcham Road, London SW17 9PG.
Tel: 020 8682 4001. Fax: 020 8682 4012.
email: info@downs-syndrome.org.uk.
www.dsa-uk.com
Educational advice and publications.

DYSLEXIA INSTITUTE

133 Gresham Road, Staines, Middlesex
TW18 2AJ. Tel: 01784 463851.
Fax: 01784 460747.
email: info@dyslexia-inst.org.uk
www.dyslexia-inst.org.uk
Assessment, information and advice.

HYPERACTIVE CHILDREN'S SUPPORT GROUP

71 Whyke Lane, Chichester, Sussex
PO19 2LD. Tel: 01243 551313.
Fax: 01243 552019.
email: hacsg@hacsg.org.uk www.hacsg.org.uk
Support for hyperactive children and
their parents.

ICAN

4 Dyer's Buildings, Holborn, London
EC1N 2QP. Tel: 0870 010 4066.
Fax: 0870 010 4067. email: ican@ican.org.uk
www.ican.org.uk
Formerly known as the Invalid Children's Aid
Nationwide. Advice, support and information
for parents of children with speech and
communication difficulties.

IPSEA

6 Carlow Mews, Woodbridge, Suffolk
IP12 1DH. Tel: 01394 380518.
www.ipsea.org.uk
The Independent Panel for Special
Education Advice. Advice to parents
from independent experts.

KIDSCAPE

2 Grosvenor Gardens, London SW1W 0DH.
Tel: 020 7730 3300. Fax: 020 7730 7081.
www.kidscape.org.uk/kidscape
Information and advice for children.
Telephone counselling for parents.

MENCAP

123 Golden Lane, London EC1 0RT.
Tel: 020 7454 0454.
www.mencap.org.uk
email: information@mencap.org.uk
This is a national charity, providing advice and
support to people with learning disabilities and
their families.
- offers help and advice about
  special schooling
- information of clubs for people with
  special needs
- fund-raising ideas

THE NATIONAL AUTISTIC SOCIETY

393 City Road, London EC1V 1NG.
Tel: 020 7833 2299. Fax: 020 7833 9666.
email: nas@nas.org.uk www.nas.org.uk
Advice, information and support for parents
and professionals.

NDCS

15 Dufferin Street, London EC1Y 8UR.
Tel: 020 7490 8656. Fax: 020 7251 5020.
email: ndcs@ndcs.org.uk. www.ndcs.org.uk
National Deaf Children's Society.
Educational advice.

Appendix 3

NSPCC
42 Curtain Road, London EC2A 3NH.
Tel: 020 7825 2500. Fax: 020 7825 2525.
email: infounit@nspcc.org.uk
www.nspcc.org.uk

Oaasis
Brock House, Grigg Lane, Brockenhurst,
Hampshire SO42 7RE. Fax: 01590 622687.
email: Idurston@oaasis.co.uk
www.oaasis.co.uk
Office for Advice, Assistance, Support and
Information on Special needs.

PHAB
Summit House, Wandle Road, Croydon,
Surrey CR10 1DF. Tel: 020 8667 9443.
Fax: 020 8681 1399.
email: info@phabengland.org.uk
www.phabengland.org.uk
Physically Handicapped and Able Bodied.

RADAR
12 City Forum, 250 City Road, London
EC1V 8AF. Tel: 020 7250 3222.
Fax: 020 7250 0212.
email: radar@radar.org.uk www.radar.org.uk
Royal Association for Disability and
Rehabilitation. Information and publications.

RATHBONE
Churchgate House, 56 Oxford Street,
Manchester M1 6EU. Tel: 0161 236 5358.
Fax: 0161 2386356.
email: info@rathbonetraining.co.uk
www.rathci-ho.demon.co.uk
Formerly known as the Rathbone Society.
Advice and support for families
and professionals.

RNIB
224 Great Portland Street, London W1N 6AA.
Tel: 020 7388 1266. Fax: 020 7288 2034.
email: helpline@rnib.org.uk www.rnib.org.uk
The Royal National Institute for the Blind.
Publications and educational advice.

RNID
19–23 Featherstone Street, London
EC1Y 8SL. Tel: 020 7296 8001.
Fax: 020 7296 8199.
email: informationline@rnid.org.uk
www.rnid.org.uk
Royal National Institute for Deaf People.
Publications and educational advice.

SCOPE
6 Market Road, London N7 9PW.
Tel: 0808 800 3333.
email: cphelpline@scope.org.uk
www.scope.org.uk
Support, information and publications for
families affected by cerebral palsy.

SENSE
11–13 Clifton Terrace, Finsbury Park,
London N4 3SR. Tel: 020 7272 7774.
Fax: 020 7272 6012.
email: enquiries@sense.org.uk
www.sense.org.uk
The National Deaf/Blind and Rubella
Association. Educational advice for parents of
children with visual and hearing impairment.

Publications

Useful resources are available from MENCAP
at the address above.

Special Educational Needs – a guide for parents
- this booklet, aimed at parents, explains special educational needs
- covers ages 2 to 16
- educational assessments and statements explained

Everybody's different schools pack (and teachers' notes)
- introduction to learning disability for children aged 9–14 years.
- teachers' notes linked to the National Curriculum are available to accompany the schools pack

For children

The Trouble with Josh: What it is Like to be Different by Carolyn Nystrome (1989)
Available from Lion Publishing, Mayfield House, 256 Banbury Road, Oxford OX2 5DH.

I have Down's Syndrome by Brenda Pettenuzzo (1987)
Available from Watts Publishing Group, 96 Leonard Street, London EC2A 4RH.
Tel: 020 7739 2929. Fax: 020 7739 2318.
www.wattspub.co.uk

Jessy Runs Away by Rachel Anderson and Shelagh McNicholas (1988)
Available from A & C Black (Publishers) Ltd. 37 Soho Square, London W1D 3QZ.
Tel: 020 7758 0200. Fax: 020 7758 0222
www.acblack.co.uk

✦ Alzheimer's Disease

Organisation

ALZHEIMER'S SOCIETY
Gordon House, 10 Green Coat Place, London SW1P 1PH. Tel: 020 7306 0606.
Helpline: 0845 300 0336 8:30am–6:30pm Mon–Fri. www.alzheimers.org.uk
email: enquiries@alzheimers.org.uk
Alzheimer's Disease society supports those who are caring for someone with dementia by offering support, advice about dementia and information on where to find help.

Publications

Suitable for children from 5 to 12 years.

'It's me Grandma! It's me!' by Eileen Evans (1991)
Available from the Bridgeport branch of the Alzheimer's Society, 5 Kings Square, Bridgeport, Dorset BT6 3QE.
Tel: 01308 420800.

Further reading may also be available from your local library.

✦ Young carers

A young carer could be from any background. Most care for their parents, but some may be taking responsibility for
- a grandparent
- sibling
- other family member.

Young carers have their lives restricted because of the need to look after a person. These children are often silent about their extent of caring, through fear of separation, guilt, pride and a desire to keep it in the family, but there are many organisations that can help these children to lead easier lives.

Organisations

CARERS UK
Ruth Pitter House, 20–25 Glasshouse Yard, London EC1A 4JT. Tel: 020 7490 8818.
Carers Line: 0808 808 7777.
www.carersuk.demon.co.uk
email: info@ukcarers.org

For Wales please contact
River House, Ynysbridge Court, Gwaelod-y-Garth, Cardiff CF15 9SS.
Tel: 029 2081 1370.

Appendix 3

NATIONAL YOUTH ADVOCACY SERVICE

1 Downham Road South, Heswall, Wirral, Merseyside CH60 5RG. Tel: 0151 342 7852. Fax: 0151 342 3174. Email: help@nyas.net
www.nyas.net
Freephone: 0800 616101 (hours 3:30 pm to 9:30 pm weekdays and 2:00 pm to 8:00 pm at weekends)

- an organisation to find the best way to help solve your problems
- makes sure that all young people have the chance to get their views across and their voices heard
- confidential service
- provides young people with an advocate
- telephone counsellors available to help

CROSSROADS CARE

10 Regent Place, Rugby, Warwickshire CV21 2PN. Tel: 01788 573 653.
www.crossroads.org.uk
Another organisation that supports carers of all ages who look after someone who has a disability.

- offers practical weekly assistance by providing care attendants to relieve the carers

There are many other organisations and associations that may be able to help.

Other people who you may have easy access to could be

- occupational therapists
- youth workers/social workers
- home care services
- family doctor

Publications

Couldn't Care More by Jenny Frank (1995)

Available from the Children's Society, Publications Department, Edward Rudolf House, Margery Street, London WC1X 0JL. Tel: 020 7841 4400.

A good source of publications on young carers is the Young Carers Research Group, based at Loughborough University, who can be contacted on 01509 223379 or via the main Loughborough website at www.lboro.ac.uk.

A sample of those available are listed below.

Children Who Care by Dr Saul Becker et al (1993)

My Child, My Carer: The Parent's Perspective by Dr Saul Becker et al (1994)

Young Carers and their families by Becker et al (1998)

Young Carers in the UK – a Profile (1998)

Young Carers in their own words edited by Andrew Bibby and Dr Saul Becker (2000)

Getting It Right For Young Carers (1994) – a training pack for professionals

In addition, the following organisations may be useful in helping to source books on sensitive issues for different reading ages and abilities.

The Reading and Language Information Centre

Bulmershe Court, Woodlands Avenue, Reading RG6 1HY. Tel: 0118 931 8820.

REACH (The national advice centre for children with reading difficulties)

Wellington House, Wellington Road, Wokingham, Berkshire RG40 2AG.
Tel: 01189 931 8820.

Books for Students

Bird Road, Heathcote, Warwick CV34 6TB.
Tel: 01926 436436.